RIDLEY BEETON

OLIVE SCHREINER

A SHORT GUIDE TO HER WRITINGS

HUMAN SCIENCES RESEARCH COUNCIL
PUBLICATION SERIES NO. 47

HOWARD TIMMINS
CAPE TOWN
1974

ISBN 0 86978 101 4

Printed by Citadel Press, Lansdowne, Cape

For Zelda

CONTENTS

	Acknowledgements and Preface	9
I.	INTRODUCTION	11
II.	NOVELS	
	The Story of an African Farm	19
	Undine	29
	Trooper Peter Halket of Mashonaland	34
	From Man to Man	37
III.	SHORT STORIES	
	Dream Life and Real Life	44
	Stories, Dreams and Allegories	44
IV.	DREAMS	
	Dreams	48
	Stories, Dreams and Allegories	48
V.	POLITICS	
	Thoughts on South Africa	53
	An English South African's View of the Situation	66
	Closer Union	67
	Other Political Writings	70
VI.	WOMEN	
	Woman and Labour	72
VII.	LETTERS	
	The Letters of Olive Schreiner	76
	Manuscript Sources	83
	BIBLIOGRAPHY	88
	APPENDIX I: *Anthology*	
	Olive Schreiner: A Selection, edited by Uys Krige	93

APPENDIX II : *Biographical and Critical Studies*

The Life of Olive Schreiner, by S. C. Cronwright-
    Schreiner   100

Not Without Honour: The Life and Writings of
    Olive Schreiner, by Vera Buchanan-Gould   104

Olive Schreiner: A Study in Latent Meanings,
    by Marion V. Friedmann   107

Olive Schreiner: Her Friends and Times, by
    D. L. Hobman   109

Olive Schreiner: Portrait of a South African
    Woman, by Johannes Meintjes   112

ACKNOWLEDGEMENTS AND PREFACE

Several sections of the present guide have appeared before as separate pieces: the Introduction was printed as 'A Short Life of Olive Schreiner' in *Lantern* (published by the Foundation for Education, Science and Technology); the appraisal of *The Story of an African Farm* appeared in the same periodical; the description of the 'Dreams' was a contribution to *When the Heart Changes: A Garland for Olive Schreiner* (Tafelberg-uitgewers), edited by Zelda Friedlander; the Bibliography also appeared in Zelda Friedlander's book, as did four of the five notes on biographical and critical studies of Olive Schreiner; the discussion of Uys Krige's selections of the writings appeared in *Unisa English Studies* (published by the University of South Africa), and that of the letters in *Research in African Literatures* (published by the University of Texas).

I wish to thank the publishers of the periodicals and the book I have mentioned, for allowing me to use this material. I am also indebted to the Society of Authors, London (the literary representative of the Havelock Ellis estate) and Syfrets Trust, Grahamstown (the representative of the Olive Schreiner estate) for allowing me to use copyright manuscript material in Chapter VII.

Repetition in what follows was unavoidable. It is my hope, however, that the perspective supplied by the different character of each of the writings under examination will remove the impression of superfluity. Indeed, I have risked repetition because it seemed to me more important that the distinctive quality of each of Olive Schreiner's writings should emerge as fully as possible, than that an overall nicety should be achieved. Each section was planned as an independent commentary, to be read – if necessary — without reference to the remainder of the work.

R.B.

The financial assistance of The Human Sciences Research Council in connection with the publication of this work, is hereby acknowledged. Opinions expressed in this work or conclusions reached, are those of the author and must in no instance be regarded as a reflection of the opinions and conclusions of The Human Sciences Research Council.

'She was a woman; she belonged to an oppressed nation; she was poor; she was beautiful. A powerful vocation summoned her . . .'

These words were not written of Olive Schreiner; they are a description of the young Maria Slodovska by her daughter, Eve Curie. Yet they could well have been used to describe the young colonial authoress when she startled the sedate world of the nineteen-eighties with her *Story of an African Farm*, with its streaks of fervid genius and its arrogant cries in the cause of feminism. Although she was intensely proud of her English heritage, she allied herself spiritually to the Boer people, and she fought through poverty and obscurity to make herself deserving of a hearing. The portraits of the young Olive Schreiner that survive suggest the woman of 'wonderful beauty and vivacity' Edward Carpenter describes in *My Days and Dreams*.[1]

She was more interesting than any of her creations. Lyndall, Rebekah, Bertie, Undine all pale beside the personality and fire of their author. Several biographers have seen her as a bundle of contradictions. 'She never invented any character,' writes D. L. Hobman in *Olive Schreiner; her Friends and Times*, 'so magnetic and fiery, so perverse and inconsistent as her own. She was everything that was contradictory: a self-centred altruist, an individualistic Socialist, a hermit who craved for friends, a fierce and aggressive pacifist. She envied men, and therefore she exalted women; she abhorred war, yet most vehemently supported the Boers against her own countrymen; she denied God, while all her life her soul was penetrated with awareness and love of the Divine' (p. 1).

Yet these contradictions are not as paradoxical as they may appear, and several of D. L. Hobman's statements require sub-

---

1. London, Allen and Unwin, 1916, p. 227.

stantial qualification. This qualification is largely supplied by the facts of her life.

She was born in 1855 at the Wittebergen Mission Station, near what is now Lesotho; Wittebergen was one of the many places at which her missionary father served. Chroniclers are by no means agreed about how many children were born to the Schreiners: the names of twelve children, of whom several died at birth or in early childhood, are recorded by Cronwright-Schreiner in his biography. Olive Schreiner grew up in an atmosphere of child-death, an atmosphere felicitously rendered in the sketch 'A Child's Day', which she used as the 'Prelude' to her posthumously published novel *From Man to Man*. Her family and early experiences supplied her with much of her creative material; it is generally agreed, for example, that her gentle, unworldly father Gottlob Schreiner was the model for the portrait of old Otto in *The Story of an African Farm*.

She was always a precocious child, and although she had little formal schooling, she was soon devouring authors normally far beyond the range of childhood and young womanhood – Darwin, Gibbon, Herbert Spencer, to mention only a few. She had set her mind on becoming a doctor, but her medical ambitions were never to be realised; shortly after completing *The Story of an African Farm* she went to London, intent on entering a hospital as a preliminary to her studies, but asthma, which became a life-long enemy, made the rigours of medical training impossible for her. Throughout her life she retained an interest in medicine, and, indeed, in all forms of scientific, systematic inquiry.

Undine her first (but posthumously published) novel was written at about the age of eighteen; she began the book during the time she lived with her brother Theo, at the 'New Rush' diamond camp, as Kimberley was then known. 'New Rush' was only one of many places to which she was sent to live after her father's dismissal, in 1865, by the London Missionary Society for a minor infringement of its regulation forbidding private trading. The enforced nomadic existence of the young girl may well have had a permanent effect on her, reflected at its most patent, possibly, in her persistent restlessness.

She had spent much of her girlhood in the Karoo, that long stretch of bleak but compellingly beautiful country, but it was only between 1874 and 1881, when she served as governess to various Cape families, that she began in earnest to translate her fervent love of the country into writing. She is reputed to have written most of *The Story of an African Farm* in a humble outhouse bedroom on the farm 'Ganna Hoek', where she was governess to the children of the Afrikaans-speaking Fouché family. Mrs Fouché, according to popular legend, was deeply distressed to learn later in life that she had been the model for Olive Schreiner's far from flattering portrait of the coarse, heavy-breathing 'Tant Sannie'. This portrait is sometimes held up as Olive Schreiner's prevailing view of the Afrikaner woman; that this is unjust, both to Olive Schreiner and to the Afrikaner, is shown by several sympathetic portraits in her writings.[2]

Olive Schreiner's early life was one of poverty, but in 1881 her brothers and sisters – some had married well, and others were in the process of becoming notable public figures (Will Schreiner became Prime Minister of the Cape Colony) – made it possible for her to go to London to study medicine, and to find a publisher for *An African Farm*. Her pursuit of medicine, as we have seen, was ill-starred, and it seemed for a time that this would also be her fate as an author: her novel was sent from publisher to publisher until in 1883, on the advice of George Meredith (who had *nothing*, Olive angrily insisted in later life, to do with its construction) Chapman and Hall issued it under the pseudonym of 'Ralph Iron' without knowing its real authorship. The book, exotic in setting and unconventional in its attitude to marriage, found a disturbed, but largely admiring public.

The book has been the subject of much literary discussion, and by the undiscerning it has been either debunked or glorified.

2. See, for example, the discussion of 'Eighteen-Ninety-Nine' in Chapter III, and that of *Thoughts on South Africa* in Chapter V.

It has been vehemently accused or righteously defended, written up or written down. What generally is not – and should not be – disputed is that it shows the workings of a remarkable, if undisciplined, mind. It shows, too, a superb imagination, but one, it seems, with disappointing limitations.

The publication of *An African Farm* led to her meeting with Havelock Ellis, in later life a famous pioneering sexologist, the author of such books as *Studies in the Psychology of Sex* and *Man and Woman*. She confessed to an overwhelming disappointment – so intense that she had immediately to retire to shed a few bitter tears – when she first met him. But there was much to draw them together: for example, he had lived in Australian bush country very similar to the Karoo of *An African Farm* – and the closeness of their subsequent association has been the subject of much speculation. 'We were not,' writes Ellis in his autobiography *My Life*, 'what can be technically, or even ordinarily, called lovers.'[3] Olive Schreiner's letters, intense though they are, are equally inscrutable. It seems from their correspondence that Ellis proposed marriage to her, probably more than once, and that she rejected him because of her devotion to her destiny as an author, and, possibly, because she herself sensed that something – a something in her idealistic mind most necessary to the linking of a man and a woman – would be missing in their relationship. After several years of pursuit a disappointed Ellis married Edith Lees; Olive Schreiner, resolutely single, had returned to South Africa searching for peace and fulfilment, the two things perpetually elusive to her.

For a time she imagined that the warm, dry air of the Karoo would relieve her asthma, and she made her home in Matjesfontein, a small railway siding where she is reputed to have had many a heated discussion with Rhodes when his train stopped on its way to the North. But neither asthma nor her agitated mind – which induced which will never be known – granted her peace, and the remainder of her life was a series of moves from place to

3. London, Heinemann, 1940, p. 185.

place. Even marriage did not long comfort her. It has often been asked why she produced so little – in fact some people will have it, almost nothing – after *An African Farm;* I find it a matter for some wonder that she produced so much in the circumstances, and at that writing of the dimension and calibre of *Thoughts on South Africa* and *Woman and Labour*, and of such radiance as the dreams and allegories.

The letterheads of her scrawling, hurried notes bear witness to her restlessness.[4] Matjesfontein becomes Johannesburg, Johannesburg Hanover, Hanover Beaufort West, Beaufort West De Aar, De Aar London; and then the whole cycle, with some different names, seems to begin again. In many of the places in which she lived Olive Schreiner became a legend, and stories of her eccentricities and courage still have currency.

Olive, who had vowed never to marry, in 1894 decided – suddenly, it seemed to her friends – to wed a local Cradock farmer, Samuel Cron Cronwright. The reasons for this change of heart remain obscure, but two seem probable: first, her passionate desire for a child, and her growing awareness of swiftly advancing middle age; and secondly, the attraction of Cronwright himself, eight years her junior, and by all accounts a fine specimen of rugged virility. After their marriage on 16th February, the Cronwright-Schreiners – he had changed his name to appease his famous wife in her fight for equal treatment for women – settled on his farm 'Krantz Plaats'. Some months after their marriage Olive found she was to have a child, and her dreams of motherhood seemed near to realisation. And perhaps, Cronwright dreamed, motherhood would bring her the stability and contentment she had never had.

The morning after her birth the Cronwright-Schreiners' little daughter – what was to be their only child – was found dead, having suffocated during the night. Forty-year-old Olive was in despair, and for years afterwards she could not bear to look at another child for fear of recalling, and reliving, her agony of grief.

4. See Chapter VII for a further account.

The Cronwright-Schreiners were somewhat distracted, however, by the clouds of war that were beginning to loom on the horizon. They were both ardent supporters of the Boers in their struggle to keep their hard-won independence. Olive Schreiner and her husband were South African patriots long before the term 'South African' had achieved currency; they were certainly *not* opposed to their own people, as D. L. Hobman asserts: their own people and their own causes were in South Africa – here they lived, and here they attempted the attainment of their ideals, one of which was to resist oppression, even if it took the name of British Empire. Rhodes was one of the most prominent objects of their censure, and in a white heat of indignation Olive Schreiner wrote her political allegory *Trooper Peter Halket of Mashonaland*, in which she tried to expose to England his inhumane treatment of the indigenous African people, and to show just what British Imperialism could amount to in South Africa. The book, ironically enough in the light of contemporary (1960–74) politics, made little impact on the British public, and Rhodes continued to be acclaimed a national hero. Together the Cronwright-Schreiners wrote *The Political Situation*, which was read by Cronwright in Kimberley, Rhodes's stronghold. Later, in 1899, with war all but on South Africa Olive Shreiner made her last despairing, but eloquently courageous call for peace, in her pamphlet *An English South African's View of the Situation;* it availed not at all, and within months South Africa was in a state of war. Olive and her husband suffered a great deal for their stand, and their integrity earned little more than suspicion and occasional insults.

When the war ended with Great Britain the inevitable victor, Olive Schreiner continued to contribute articles on public issues. *A Letter on the Jew*, a vehement protest against anti-semitism, appeared in 1906, and *Closer Union*, a consideration of the principles that should govern a union of the four provinces, in 1908. Her greatest 'political' book *Thoughts on South Africa* appeared only after her death. In 1911 she published her famous work on feminism, *Woman and Labour*, which seems to have produced an enduring effect on notable women of subsequent decades. Vera Brittain, for example, in her autobiography *Testament of Youth* acknowledges the tremendous stimulus it gave to greater public action by women.

After the Boer war the Cronwright-Schreiners had become more and more alienated. Cronwright had sold his farm because it seemed to aggravate his wife's asthma, and for many years had continued to follow her from place to place, changing his profession, hoping to see the end of her illness and the completion of the masterpieces he had tried to encourage her to write. Although he played a long-suffering role – and much of his suffering was undoubtedly genuine – he seems at last to have been completely out of patience with a woman incurably erratic, but demanding, and often deserving, devotion and understanding.

From 1913 until a few months before her death in 1920 Olive Schreiner lived in Europe, mainly in England, finally having despaired it seems of ever completing her projected 'big' novel, *From Man to Man*, on which she worked, with an ever-increasing sense of hopelessness, for nearly forty years. The Great War of 1914–1918 added substantially to her spiritual agony and her physical discomfort, although she still spoke up heatedly and finely on subjects she held in esteem. Her German name and her campaigns in support of pacifism did little to endear her to a British public intensely and, at times, recklessly anti-German. Two years after the war the Cronwright-Schreiners were re-united in London; Olive had weakened and aged so much that Cronwright did not at first recognise her when she opened the door to him. Nevertheless, she left for South Africa a month later without him, Cronwright pleading the need for a longer rest in England.

Olive Schreiner, only three months in South Africa, died quietly in her hotel bedroom in Wynberg, Cape Town, in the early hours of 11th December, 1920. Without religious ceremony – although she retained the profoundest belief in God, she had early expressed her rebellion against orthodox Christianity – she was buried in Maitland Cemetery in Cape Town. Cronwright returned from England the following year, and in accordance with a wish Olive had expressed when they walked together on his farm during their first year of marriage, he arranged for her reburial on Buffels Kop, one of the highest points of 'Krantz Plaats'. Three coffins were taken up the koppie; the body o Olive's baby and that of her pet dog, Nita, were sealed with hers in the ironstone sarcophagus Cronwright had had built.

It has become something of a fashion, in an age which is tending to be super-intelligent, to discredit, especially when shortcomings present themselves in abundance as they did in the case of Olive Schreiner, both in her life and work. There should of course be no pretence that she was consistently sagacious – she wasn't; *Undine*, some of her short stories and political writings, and many of her letters are here to prove that.

But there *is* a case for Olive Schreiner, and a strong one. Her mind cannot be dismissed as an erratic nothing – she undoubtedly had great, and, at times, amazingly sustained intelligence. Although the application of the great love she professed was disjointed, it was certainly not insincere, and was expressed on occasion with admirable courage. Although her vision was often clouded, this is no indication that it wasn't there; it had, indeed, a forceful reality. Although she stumbled sometimes and became a pamphleteer, at her best she was a great artist and an exacting and profound thinker.

Her writings substantially prove these contentions.

THE STORY OF AN AFRICAN FARM

It was one of Olive Schreiner's tenets that life is unpredictable and that art should have this same quality. In the Preface to *The Story of an African Farm* she allies her method in the book to

the method of the life we all lead. Here nothing can be prophesied. There is a strange coming and going of feet. Men appear, act and re-act upon each other, and pass away. When the crisis comes the man who would fit it does not return. When the curtain falls no one is ready. When the footlights are brightest they are blown out; and what the name of the play is no one knows. If there sits a spectator who knows, he sits so high that the players in the gaslight cannot hear his breathing. (pp. vii–viii)[1]

This quotation takes us into her at times strangely inconsequential, but persistently attractive, 'Story'.

When the book opens night has fallen on the African farm:

The full African moon poured down its light from the blue sky into the wide, lonely plain. The dry, sandy earth, with its coating of stunted 'karroo' bushes a few inches high, the low hills that skirted the plain, the milk-bushes with their long, finger-like leaves, all were touched by a weird and an almost oppressive beauty as they lay in the white light. (p. 9)

The reader's eye is made to move carefully over the rest of the farm. But the writer's ability to touch the imagination is far more important than all the attractions she produces for the eye. By the very terms of the description we have been prepared for more than the comprehension of a setting: we travel further, into the heart of a young boy, lying awake in the wagon-house, listening

---

1. Page references in this chapter are to the 1924 edition of *The Story of an African Farm*, published in London by T. Fisher Unwin. Unless otherwise stated all page references to Olive Schreiner's works are to the first editions listed in the Bibliography.

to the ticking of his father's watch. This is Waldo, and it is through him that we have the first intimations of Olive Schreiner's doubts and agonies when he grovels before God, and beseeches Him to save humanity.

Day dawns on the African farm:

> The farm by daylight was not as the farm by moonlight. The plain was a weary flat of loose red sand, sparsely covered by dry karroo bushes, that cracked beneath the tread like tinder, and showed the red earth everywhere. Here and there a milk-bush lifted its pale-coloured rods, and in every direction the ants and beetles ran about in the blazing sand. The red walls of the farmhouse, the zinc roofs of the outbuildings, the stone walls of the 'kraals', all reflected the fierce sunlight, till the eye ached and blenched. No tree or shrub was to be seen far or near. The two sunflowers that stood before the door, out-stared by the sun, drooped their brazen faces to the sand; and the little cicada-like insects cried aloud among the stones of the 'kopje'. (pp. 13–4)

Even two short extracts such as these provide telling evidence of Olive Schreiner's mastery of description, of her ability to communicate the atmosphere of a place. The faults of *The Story of an African Farm* do not relate primarily to its style, which has been acknowledged as little short of amazing for one so young (the book was written, according to available evidence, when Olive Schreiner was in her very early twenties), but to its incessant moralising, its obsession with the cause of woman, and its inartistic grotesques. Long tracts of the book, for example, are given to unrelated moral argument. These things certainly clouded the jewel of the book's genius. Yet *An African Farm* has an intensely vital moral force, and still today provokes argument about its value and meaning.

Why has it this force? A book ill-conceived and, as some critics contend, on nearly every important count badly-executed, would have very little potency.

An African Farm was shot through with passionate, and, often, a wonderfully realised genius that rose above the importance of

20

competence, of mere talent, and, frequently, above the importance of fault. It is often compared to Emily Brontë's *Wuthering Heights*, and the comparison is not casual: although Olive Schreiner's work was in many ways (and, in most cases, unfortunately) more 'intellectual', both novels have similar constituents, as well as a pervasive spirit of untutored genius: for example, wild evocative nature, sombre, restless characters, moral revolt, cruelty, love beyond death, and beyond life.

But what – to persist – is the great merit of the book? It seems to me that it is located in its gift, at its best (and the book is often at its best), of evoking atmosphere sparingly, not by a burden of description; and of illuminating values, not by tedious tract-writing, but by the vivid embodiment of its own specific vision and 'life'. The passages I quoted earlier are not conventional background description: they are part of the whole book, part of its final statement, and require to be there as much as the most vital of the characters. When the author moves away from her intuitive mastery of 'organic' development – as she does, for example, in making Lyndall moralise tediously about the cause of woman – the texture of the book suffers and on such occasions *An African Farm* does indeed become contrived.

Fault has been found with her three main characters – Lyndall, Waldo, Em – and fault there undoubtedly is. Of the three the character of Lyndall is most at fault. Both Lyndall and Waldo are aspects of Olive Schreiner's own nature. There is much less trace of the author in the character of Em, and Em, possibly because of this distancing, is a near-perfect creation. The better side of Olive went into the creation of Waldo: he has her deep instinctive feel-ings and her bewildering regions of darkness. Lyndall was more her mouthpiece, expressing as she does Olive Schreiner's views on feminism – not always ineffectively, but seldom in keeping with the girl's age or with the situations in which she is constrained to give utterance to them. The child Lyndall is a fearless and enchanting creature, perhaps a little cold-blooded; the sixteen-year-old 'woman' who returns from college filled with the evan-gelism of her sex is far less compelling, and, for this reason, far less interesting, although our emotions are still at times touched, as they are when she cries out on one occasion:

> 'I am so weary of myself! . . . I want to love! I want something great and pure to lift me to itself! . . . I am so cold, so hard, so hard; will no one help me?' (p. 270)

Lyndall's main interest for us is in the devotion she stirs in the heart of Waldo. At times there is the suggestion of a deep essential bond between them although this is never so powerfully realised as the bond between Heathcliff and Cathy in *Wuthering Heights*.

> She rested her cheek softly against his shoulder. 'When I am with you I never know that I am a woman and you are a man; I only know that we are both things that think. Other men when I am with them, whether I love them or not, they are mere bodies to me; but you are a spirit . . .' p. (231)

Their tie is not essentially, or even at all, sexual; it is elemental. Lyndall is lost to Waldo in the arms of another man, but to the end, in some unexpressed, but convincing way, they retain their hold on each other.

> ' . . . if I should not,' Lyndall replies, when Waldo asks her to write to him, 'you can still remember, wherever you are, that you are not alone' (p. 248).

I have suggested that Lyndall and Waldo show two sides of Olive Schreiner's character. They reveal the two kinds of issue with which she grappled all her life: Lyndall is concerned with practical matters – the inadequacy of the conventions, the question of labour, the position of women; Waldo is concerned with more elemental questions – death, God, the meaning and purpose of life. Both are hopelessly impractical, as Olive Schreiner herself was, but Lyndall shows more the exterior side of her creator, and Waldo shows the inner side.

Their very different natures are beautifully contrasted in their conversation at Tant' Sannie's wedding as they lie in the wagon under the stars.

> 'It does not matter what you choose . . .' Lyndall tells Waldo, 'but know your aim and live for that one thing. We have only one life. The secret of success is concentration . . .'

'Yes,' says Waldo, some time later, 'but when we lie and think, and think, we see that there is nothing worth doing. The universe is so large, and man so small . . .'

She replies: 'But we must not think so far; it is madness, it is a disease' (pp. 238–40).

On Lyndall's death the old questions rise up overwhelmingly in Waldo; in the apparent meaninglessness of her end he questions the meaning of life. He works through all the old accepted creeds, all the old conventional interpretations of the purpose of existence, and he searches desperately for assurance that the individual soul is immortal. As his creator herself did earlier in the book he must, for the sake of his willingness to live deeply, come to the conclusion that existence is 'not a chance jumble; [but] a living thing, a *One*' (p. 157). 'For the soul,' Olive Schreiner comments, 'which knows itself no more as a unit, but as a part of the Universal Unity of which the Beloved also is a part; which feels within itself the throb of the Universal Life; for that soul there is no death' (p. 333).

The relation between Em and Waldo, again non-sexual, is expressed with delicate artistry. In the chapter 'Waldo goes out to taste life, and Em stays at home and tastes it', we read:

> At nine o'clock in the evening, packing his bundles for the next morning's start, Waldo looked up, and was surprised to see Em's yellow head peeping in at his door . . . She said she had made him sandwiches for his journey, and she stayed a while to help him put his goods into the saddle-bags.
>
> 'You can leave the old things lying about,' she said; 'I will lock the room, and keep it waiting for you to come back some day.'
>
> To come back some day! Would the bird ever return to its cage? But he thanked her. (p. 244)

He does come back, because he is compelled to turn to something that reminds him of Lyndall. In a night of storm Em sits by herself, Gregory Rose having left in pursuit of the woman he now loves desperately, when she hears a knocking at the door.

She opened the door a little way, and held the light behind her to defend it from the wind. The figure of a tall man stood there, and before she could speak he had pushed his way in, and was forcing the door to close behind him.

'Waldo!' she cried in astonishment. (p. 279)

He asks about Lyndall, but Em's replies are evasive. As she prepares something for him to eat he sits down and writes to Lyndall, telling her where he has been, how he has worked with labourers and struggled beside wagon-oxen, been cheated and sneered at, and how he has reacted darkly, hardly comprehending, against what was shoddy.

He writes and writes. In the following scene he is eventually interrupted by Em, who has slept while he has been writing.

She rose slowly after a time, and rested her hand on his shoulder.

'You have many letters to write,' she said.

'No,' he answered; 'it is only one to Lyndall.'

She turned away, and stood long before the fire looking into it . . .

'Waldo, dear,' she said, putting her hand on his, 'leave off writing.'

He threw back the dark hair from his forehead and looked at her.

'It is no use writing any more,' she said.

'Why not?' he asked . . .

'Waldo,' she said, 'Lyndall is dead.' (p. 297)

Some days afterwards Waldo goes out to sit in the sun with the chickens and does not wake up, and, with a coda effect, the story has ended. We feel, though it is never stated crudely in the book, that he has gone to join Lyndall.

From the boy who lay awake in the darkness, who decided that he hated God but loved Jesus, who 'lay on his stomach on the red sand' (p. 158), who carved a piece of wood which was his incoherent expression of his search for truth, who grew up into a strong, undemanding man, who worked and suffered with the beasts – Waldo is, in all the terms he commands, a finely

24

credible creation, perhaps the finest in Olive Schreiner's fiction.

The portrait of Em, the plain, unquestioning cousin of Lyndall and stepdaughter of the old Boer woman, is deeply felt and unmistakably 'genuine'; for the reader she emerges as a compellingly true daughter of the silent Karoo. Em embodies the qualities of unselfishness, gentleness and kindness without being irritating. She has none of the intellectual pretensions of Lyndall, none of the dark shadows of Waldo, but she has her own sad little story, subsidiary to those of the other main characters. She is not, it seems, fitted for the leading role, but is complementary.

'What is Em like . . . ?' Gregory Rose asks Lyndall.

'The accompaniment of a song,' she replies. 'She fills up the gaps in other people's lives, and is always number two; but I think she is like many accompaniments – a great deal better than the song she is to accompany.' (p. 257)

Exception has been taken to the portrait of Tant' Sannie, Em's stout, snoring stepmother; several critics have felt that Olive Schreiner intended her to be typical of the Boer woman, but those who have read *Thoughts on South Africa* will know that this is simply not so. Other critics, looking perhaps slightly more deeply, have made much of the 'fact' that while in her polemical writings Olive Schreiner expressed sympathy for the Boers, in her creative work she was destructively critical. It must be remembered, however, that her minor half-comic characters, and the Boer people of her fiction were usually such, had half-comic originals, people who possessed the authentic and colourful rusticity she required.[2] And the fact is continually overlooked that she could and did draw Afrikaner people of great quality, for example the very fine Boer mother in the short story 'Eighteen-Ninety-Nine', a fictional embodiment of Olive's admiration for the Boer people, and particularly the Boer woman.

Whatever may be argued about the intention of the portrait, the fact remains that Tant' Sannie is a superbly executed minor character. Though often crude and intemperate, she also has

2. The discussion on p. 13 is relevant.

flashes of kindness and humour. The keen eye and the smile with which she is so often observed defeat the arguments of those who see nothing in her but an embodiment of anti-Boer cynicism: her scene with a young suitor, her 'upsitting', is excellent comedy, and the description of her Boer wedding, though objective, is certainly not conceived in a spirit of malice.

The portrait of Bonaparte Blenkins, on the other hand, is not much more than clumsy caricature; it is too sharp-edged, too lacking in warmth. He has far too few human faculties, and emerges as an over-blatant instrument of his writer's purpose. To some extent Olive Schreiner recognised her failure. 'I agree with you in objecting to Bonaparte,' she wrote to Havelock Ellis; ' . . . he is drawn closely after life, but in hard straight lines without shading, and is not artistic . . .' (*The Letters of Olive Schreiner*, p. 12). But if his portrait has too much edge to it, the edge to his malice bestows on him some sort of jerky life (and perhaps gives the book just the drop of acid it requires).

In the scene that follows Waldo arrives at the farm, having been away at the mill for some days. He is greeted by Bonaparte:

> 'Good-morning, my dear boy. Where are you running to so fast with your rosy cheeks?'
>
> The boy looked up at him, glad even to see Bonaparte.
>
> 'I am going to the cabin,' he said, out of breath.
>
> 'You won't find them in just now – not your good old father,' said Bonaparte.
>
> 'Where is he?' asked the lad.
>
> 'There beyond the camps,' said Bonaparte, waving his hand oratorically towards the stone-walled ostrich camps.
>
> 'What is he doing there?' asked the boy.
>
> Bonaparte patted him on the cheek kindly.
>
> 'We could not keep him any more, it was too hot. We've buried him, my boy,' said Bonaparte, touching with his finger the boy's cheek. 'We couldn't keep him any more. He, he, he!' laughed Bonaparte, as the boy fled away along the low stone wall . . . (p. 88)

The little touches in the passage show the skill and insight of the born writer: the kind pat, for example, has a subtly chilling, and sickening, effect.

Although exasperatingly long-suffering, old Otto, Waldo's father, has at times an air of great conviction; he is based on Olive's remembrance of her own father, Gottlob Schreiner. Otto is paid evil for good, cruelty for kindness, and this particular aspect of the author's picture of human relations is frightening and somewhat repellent. Will he have his reward in heaven? We cannot know, and the writer refuses to speculate. (We cannot help wishing that he had just a little more of it on earth.) His likeness, yet unlikeness, to his son is delicately rendered, with Olive Schreiner's finest intuitive feeling for character; it is only when she over-plans her portraits, as in Lyndall and Bonaparte, that her pen falters.

Gregory Rose's is a puzzling portrait. The scenes in which he disguises himself as a female nurse in his effort to win Lyndall's dependence and some form of regard for him are among the strangest in Olive Schreiner's repertoire. They do nothing to diminish the enigma of the book, but one is oddly reluctant to dismiss them on the grounds of improbability. His petulant, revealing letters to his sister prepare us for these later scenes, and we are made to feel poignantly the turning away of his affection for Em and his reluctant, driven love for Lyndall. Lyndall goes away in the arms of a lover, and although she ridicules and despises him, Gregory must follow.

He tells Em he must leave the farm.

'Are you going to your friends?' she asks.

'Look here, Em,' he says between his teeth, 'I can't stand it any more. I am going to her.' (p. 275)

He cannot be other than he is: although he is weak and effeminate, he is thrust on hopelessly by the almost inhuman power of his love for Lyndall.

In an earlier scene he asks her:

'And what do you think I am like?'

'Like a tin duck,' Lyndall replies, 'floating on a dish of water, that comes after a piece of bread stuck on a needle, and the more the needle pricks it the more it comes on.' (p. 257)

Fate is perverse and inscrutable for the people who live on the African farm, as it was, in some measure, for their creator all her life. But despite the vacillations and stabs of fortune, the goal Olive saw and strove for is never lost sight of in the book. Her white bird, truth, stays steadfastly before her as she works through the story's misadventures.

Waldo's father dies. Waldo himself is cruelly ill-treated; he is lonely, destitute, without any form of assurance.

'There is no God!' he hisses desperately to Lyndall, 'no God; not anywhere!' (p. 93)

Yet he must, perforce, grow up and recognise some measure of authority in the world in which he lives. Later in the book we find him carving a piece of wood, making it as beautiful as his powers allow, trying in it to reveal something as yet ungrasped, a record of some deep unavailing search. A stranger comes to the farm, sees Waldo's carving and relates to him the allegory of the bird of truth. The stranger departs and Waldo's dark, searching life continues; he leaves the farm, does unsatisfying work in the towns, like Olive Schreiner herself moves restlessly from place to place; he undertakes the work of beasts, bears their burden – ever searching. He returns at last to the African farm for Lyndall, to be told that she is dead. There is nothing more, and he himself dies in the sunlight. This seems so much a story of blind groping and frustration, of missed chances and abortive attempts at understanding, and yet the allegory of the white bird underlies the unexpectedly powerful surge of the book.[3] Waldo's failures do not greatly depress us because we remember the bird and its silver feather – truth has been present in his life, and somewhere, somehow he has known. His reward has been small, but it is enough. To give vitality to such a proposition undoubtedly requires more than a stroke of genius.

Is it all written here, in this book, Olive Schreiner's record of a pilgrim's progress towards truth?

3. See also p. 50.

'Certainly,' says the stranger, speaking of his allegory to Waldo, 'the whole of the story is not written here, but it is suggested. And the attribute of all true art, the highest and the lowest, is this – that it says more than it says, and takes you away from itself.' (p. 177)

I want this quotation to serve as my own estimate of the value of *The Story of an African Farm*.

UNDINE

It is hardly fair to assess *Undine* critically, for Olive Schreiner never wished her first novel to be published. In fact, in her correspondence we have evidence that she asked Havelock Ellis to return the manuscript to her so that she could destroy it. She probably realised its immaturities, and what novel by an author probably in her teens would not be immature? It is only because Ellis failed to comply with her request that the novel has survived.

Yet the book undoubtedly has merit. It cannot be as swiftly despatched as Marion Friedmann attempts to do by calling it 'undeniably poor stuff' (p. 1). D. L. Hobman's reference to it as 'novelettish' (p. 58) is less unjust, although scarcely adequate. A work which contains writing of the quality of the following extract hardly deserves such sweeping dismissal:

> High on the western bank of the stream against the white, dreamy evening sky, the branches of the oliven-trees were visible, with pale, quivering, up-pointed leaves. All the dark trees around lay glittering and motionless, but the air stirred those pale green, upward-pointing leaves till they shook against the still white night sky; and on Undine, as she stood looking up at it, a great hush came and a great joy; for heaven is not a long way off, nor the beautiful for which we thirst. She dropped the pinafores she held in her hand and knelt down on the smooth white sand, and when she rose, just above the treetops the first star was shining. (pp. 191–2)[4]

4. Page references are to the Ernest Benn 1929 edition, published in London.

The book, undeniably, is riddled with weaknesses and gaucher-
ies; it is not a first-class work of fiction by any means. Even at a
superficial level, constant use of contractions such as ' 'twas' and
' 'tis' weaken the style (though it is possible that the writer would
have excluded these had she revised the text), and passages such
as the following, posed to represent profound thought, are clearly
immature: 'The untruth . . . passed from her lips to bring forth
the poisoned fruit which the lie bears, be it spoken for God's glory
or the salvation of a soul'. (p. 105) A large section of the novel (I
am thinking mainly of the part set in England) is unrealistic,
melodramatic and dull. The writer at such times seems to have
lost her gift for graphic and precise description; when set beside
her very assured evocations of Africa, the rendering of England
seems permeated by her ignorance.

Although the material is at times similar, the style on the whole
is hardly the style of *The Story of an African Farm*. Compare the
following description of the Karoo with those in the justly more
famous book:

Karoo, red sand, great mounds of round iron-stones, and
bushes never very beautiful to look at and now almost burned
into the ground by the blazing summer's sun. An old Dutch
farmhouse built of the brightest red brick to match the
ground and stones; an old stone wall broken down here and
there at irregular intervals, as if to allow for the ready in-
gress and egress of the hundred enterprising goats, whose
delight it is daily to regale themselves on the deformed peach-
trees and leafless cabbage stalks which the enclosure contains; an old tent-wagon, whose tent and floor have long
gone the way of all flesh – wood flesh – into the fire; an
ancient willow-tree, which stands vainly trying to reflect
itself in a small pond of thick red fluid, and under which
may at all times be seen a couple of dirty and benighted
ducks, who there disport themselves under the happy de-
lusion of its being water.

All these parts compose a picture in which, when looked
at by daylight, it were hard work to find the slightest trace

of beauty; but to-night, penetrated in every nook and corner by the cold white light of an almost full moon, there is a strange, weird beauty, a beauty which the veriest sheep-souled Boer that ever smoked pipe or wore vel-skoen might feel if he had but one ray of light left in him. (p. 13)

This is little more than a catalogue of features: the high quality of 'integration' and, consequently, the impelling atmosphere of the Karoo evoked in *An African Farm*, are almost totally lacking.

The character of Undine herself is substantially a failure: she is too romantically generous, too needlessly suffering, too mis-understood – obviously the creation of a very young, and an imaginatively self-indulgent, person. (The early Undine, how-ever, emerges as a charming creature, much more real in every way than the woman she becomes.)

The other principal portraits are even less successful.

But some of the minor characters, particularly unpleasant women, are humorously and sparingly evoked, though their descriptions are, perhaps, too emphatically overlaid by caricature. Undine's governess in the first chapter is described as 'this indi-vidual' who 'wore three curls on each side of her head and carried a large wart on the tip of her chin' (p. 15). Her 'ideas were so truly correct, feminine, and orthodox, that they might all have been placed in an ordinary breakfast saucer and left there for ever, without the least fear of their ever running over' (p. 20). This is almost a Dickensian portrait, with its sharp, telling strokes. The description of the gossipy Miss Mell is also vivid in the Dickensian sense: ' "Beautiful!" said Miss Mell, with a sharpen-ing in her voice that made it very fit company for her nose' (p. 41).

Mrs Snappercaps, who makes her appearance later in the novel, firmly takes her place as the arch-priestess of this strange assembly. The young Olive Schreiner was possessed of a satiric humour and a sense of grotesquerie that have the same angular vividness in her depiction of Mrs Snappercaps as they do in that of Bonaparte Blenkins in *The Story of an African Farm*. Mrs Snappercaps's re-ligious service for the benefit of her husband and Undine attain a funniness that borders on the macabre.

The following passage is an example of the writer's early method:

> Undine took the book out; Mrs Snappercaps took it up.
>
> ' "Spencer's *First Principles*." Who wrote these sermons?' asked Mrs Snappercaps.
>
> 'Spencer,' said Undine.
>
> 'Spencer, of course; I know that,' said Mrs Snappercaps, perceiving for the first time that Spencer was the name of the author and not of the book. 'Of course I know his name's Spencer, but who is he? What is he? What does he believe?'
>
> 'I shall be glad to lend you the book,' said Undine, 'if you care to read it.'
>
> 'Not unless I know who he was,' said Mrs Snappercaps . . . (p. 182)

It is difficult to believe that Olive Schreiner was only about eighteen when she wrote the following passage. The governess of the three curls and the wart is instructing Undine and two young Dutch girls:

> The chapter chosen for their perusal and consideration was the twenty-fifth of Matthew, and when it was concluded each was in turn required to ask some questions bearing on its contents. The eldest of the Dutch girls – on whom the heat, the darkness of the room, and the exertion of spelling out the long English words had had an almost stupefying effect – sat for some moments gazing at the face of her oracle with an expression of hopeless vacancy. At length a happy thought occurred to her: Were the virgins men or women? The mental effort required for the birth of this question seemed so completely to have exhausted all her powers of mind as to make it highly probable that the reply of the oracle was lost upon her, and that she remained for ever in total ignorance on the momentous subject of her inquiry. (pp. 22–3)

Throughout the novel Olive Schreiner tilts at religion, which she associates with a nauseating hypocrisy. All her more unpleasant characters – Miss Mell, Undine's grandfather, Mrs Goodman, Mrs Snappercaps – practise formal religion, puffing themselves out with a self-righteousness that almost invariably conceals malice. They are quite without the desire to examine the implications of their faith. Undine despises 'such things as revival meetings, and good people who always say one thing and mean another . . .' (p. 45)

'Go to chapel,' Mrs Barnacles advises Undine, 'and give up reading those nonsensical books, and act like other people, even if you don't think like them . . . You'll repent it if you don't.' The young author comments: ' . . . Undine, half bitter, half indifferent, would get away from her to the dear old world of inanimate nature, which never calls us queer and strange, or advises us to wear a mask'. (p. 66)

Undine, like Olive herself, was in actuality deeply religious, was constantly exploring and pondering biblical revelation. She acts according to the dictate of an imperative instinct, even if it should lead her into the way of pain: ' . . . she would go to chapel no more . . . she could not go, she thought; and wondered wearily if she were always to be afflicted with senses of duty driving her into paths where no one else would or could walk' (p. 48). 'All people who love Christ,' she tells her grandfather, 'should keep away from such places, which only bring disgrace and shame upon His name . . . It's all a mockery and an empty show, and I shall never go again, never, never!' (p. 55). The novel deals largely with man's injustice to man, or, more substantially, woman's injustice to woman, and it is from the formally religious persons of the novel that much of this injustice emanates. One leaves the book with the impression that most people in the writer's childhood world were unbelievably dreary, miserable specimens.

Like Olive Schreiner herself, and like most of her principal characters – Lyndall, Waldo and Bertie – Undine is persistently unsettled; the novel is pervaded by this sense of restlessness as the girl moves from place to place, from the Karoo farm to a rather unreal England, then to the diamond mines of South Africa, in the course of her wanderings always savouring and exploring what seems to be 'life'.

Yet for all her travels the mystery of existence continues to be a defeating experience. The child Undine who told her pet monkey Socrates 'I wish we knew' (p. 14), is instructed on her death by the star above her: 'I know nothing . . . and what you are, or I am . . . I cannot tell, and what we mean I cannot tell . . .' (p. 253).

Although life remains a mystery and the human personality persists as a secret, each person has it in his power to make a new contribution to the sum of existence. Though endeavour has its frustrations, it also has its excitement: '. . . where one soul stands, never has stood, and never shall stand, another; . . . each man's life and struggle is a mystery, incomprehensible and for ever hid from every heart but his own' (p. 56). That a person as young as the writer then was should have thought these thoughts is not in itself remarkable, but what is remarkable is that she was able to express them so succinctly.

TROOPER PETER HALKET OF MASHONALAND

Trooper Peter Halket of Mashonaland is not really a novel at all. It is in many ways nearer to Olive Schreiner's allegories, although, again, it does not possess their detachment. It is hardly more than propaganda written in a white heat of emotion against Rhodes and the evils his Chartered Company were perpetrating in the name of the British Empire. It was intended for immediate effect rather than as enduring artistic expression – needless to say the writer's fulminations (for on occasion they are not much more than this) did little damage to the already tarnished but still popular image of Rhodes as a great corner-stone of the British Empire and of British honour.

The book lacks the interesting construction of a novel; it has not much more than a simple plot on which the propaganda is hoisted. And yet it is a novel in that it fulfils the basic requirements: it is of the requisite minimum length, it is a fiction except in its imputations, it tells a story, in some measure it creates character.

Trooper Peter Halket of the Chartered Company's forces in Rhodesia has lost his troop and settles down to spend the night by himself on a koppie in the Rhodesian bush. He has no fears: his comrades will find him in the morning; the surrounding native tribes have been thoroughly crushed. He falls to pleasant meditating about his mother at home, the black women he has enjoyed in Rhodesia, the natives he has slaughtered, the money he will make by dispossessing the black people and by taking in gullible overseas investors. Then he hears a step, and his flesh suddenly creeps with terror. 'Who is there?' he cries out. A voice answers: 'A friend' (p. 44). He is joined by a man, a Jew, dressed in a simple linen garment, whom we have little difficulty in recognising as Christ, although this identity is never actually stated. He speaks to Peter Halket, telling him stories (in a manner that would seem gauche and artless in hands other than Olive Schreiner's) about sincere, noble people. The evil of his pursuits soon becomes apparent to the young Trooper. Having imparted faith and principle to him, the Jew departs into the night, leaving him to himself on the koppie.

The next morning he is found by his troop, defies the captain, who has been torturing a captured native intended for execution the following morning. During the night Peter Halket is shot down by the captain when attempting to free the native, and he is buried by his troop in the Rhodesian veld. A comrade looks back at the grave as the soldiers ride off and comments: 'I hardly know ... whether it is not better for him now, than for us'. (p. 264)

That is all. Trooper Halket's conversion takes place with the swiftness of the allegory, but Olive's depiction of him is not wholly inadequate. 'He was a slight man of middle height,' she describes him, 'with a sloping forehead and pale blue eyes: but the jaws were hard set, and the thin lips of the large mouth were those of a man who could strongly desire the material good of life, and enjoy it when it came his way' (pp. 18–9). About his character we are told: 'As a rule he lived in the world immediately about him, and let the things of the moment impinge on him, and fall off again as they would, without much reflection'. (p. 23) He plans to make money out of syndicate shares floated on promises, but his is not mere rascality. He is saturated by the insensitivity his way of life has encouraged: 'And then the other people, that bought the shares for cash! Well, they could sell out too; they could *all* sell out!' (p. 33). In his conversation with the stranger he reveals both sensuality and cruelty. 'One girl was only fifteen,' he tells the stranger. 'I got her cheap from a policeman who was living with her, and she wasn't much. But the other, by God! I never saw another nigger like her . . .' (p. 57). And: 'I've potted as many niggers as any man in our troop, I bet'. (p. 79) Native women are sold for kegs of brandy; native men are hanged from trees on the slightest pretext. The young Trooper epitomises, not so much the cruelty, as that state of mindlessness that not only allows such conditions to continue, but actively assists them. (In this, of course, there is a fable for our own time – the writer's propaganda is not entirely dated.)[5]

We are now asked to accept that a great change, a reformation, overtakes his character. The stranger talks to him, shows him the evil conditions that abound in Rhodesia, and we are to believe that Trooper Halket returns to his camp a militant evangelist, an unhesitating champion of the downtrodden. This sudden change may not meet those demands for credibility that seem intrinsic to the novel as a literary form; yet we must remember that the writer was here not primarily concerned with the

5. The Rhodesian difficulties of the nineteen-sixties and seventies, as well as the advent to power in 1948 of the National Party in South Africa, have brought us closer to the propagandist aspect of the work, though it would be foolish to pretend that the problems with which Olive Schreiner deals and those that confront us are identical.
The 1959 Paperback Edition (London, Ernest Benn Limited) contains an introduction by Trevor Huddleston; in it he describes Olive Schreiner, accurately, as a precursor of modern liberal thinking in Africa – her attitude could, conceivably, give light to the present anti-racial struggles taking place in Africa.

development of the novel's possibilities, but with delivering a message its form seemed to admit. There is in this at least a compelling immediacy of purpose. The stuttering, awkward way in which Halket delivers himself of the message imparted by the stranger (in turn, reaching our ears by way of some of the soldiers who witnessed the scene) is not, however, inconsistent with his character, and shows that even Olive Schreiner, the pamphleteer, could retain the qualities of a thoughtful artist.

Even in this minor book she often attains excellence when evoking atmosphere, in this case the heavy silence of the Rhodesian bush. The young Trooper is uneasy amidst this absence of familiar sounds. Suddenly he starts and listens. 'But it was only the wind coming up the kopje like a great wheezy beast creeping upwards . . .' (p. 29). Next day, the central African heat returns: 'The sun poured down its rays over the scattered trees, and stunted bush, and long grass, and over the dried up river beds' (p. 193). Though Olive Schreiner's characterisation and plot may suffer because of the propaganda with which she has decided to weight the book, her atmosphere, her backdrop of Rhodesia, seldom fails.

The message – although we cannot from our place in time fully appreciate the circumstances that made her give such urgent voice to it – is at least strikingly unequivocal.

FROM MAN TO MAN

For over forty years Olive Schreiner worked spasmodically on her last novel *From Man to Man*. Throughout those forty years a more appropriate title for her book constantly suggested itself to her: from *Other Men's Sins* she changed to *A Small Bit of Mimosa* and *Wrecked*, then to *Saints and Sinners*, and finally to *From Man to Man;* towards the end of her life she considered calling it *Perhaps Only*.[6] The book was constantly revised, parts of it destroy-

6. These changes of title are based on the evidence collected by Cronwright-Schreiner and brought together by him at the beginning of the book.

ed, other parts built up again. It has been suggested that Olive Schreiner was not essentially a creative writer because of her mystifying inability to complete this book. Again and again she promises herself that she will end off *From Man to Man*, buafter her death the conclusion had to be supplied by her hustband.

A key to the mystery of the book's incompletion is perhaps located in the irony that this was to be her most complete statement. It was to be her summation, in an artistic form, of life as she saw it – she could never quite bring herself to that statement because she was constantly realising how patchy her comprehension was. 'I wish,' she writes to Havelock Ellis about the book, 'I wish I had more power; I would put it all into this book; I would write so that no one who read it shall ever forget it' (*The Letters of Olive Schreiner*, p. 16). She was always struggling towards the statement, but never quite reaching it, and it may well have been her grand, despairing realisation that 'perhaps only God knew what the lights and shadows were' (this appears, in a facsimile of her own handwriting, on the title page of the book, indicating the importance her husband attached to the statement). *From Man to Man* must therefore be accepted as a seriously incomplete manifesto, but by no means valueless for that reason. (We have in fact become accustomed to authoritative statements by considerably lesser talents and they have all too often been drearily self-confident.)

From Man to Man does not contain the fire or genius of *The Story of an African Farm*, although the prelude entitled 'The Child's Day' is, in its way, as good as anything Olive Schreiner ever wrote, and, within its limitations of form and characterisation, equal to almost any piece of creative writing to emerge from South Africa:

> The little mother lay in the agony of child-birth. Outside all was still but the buzzing of the bees, some of which now and then found their way in to the half darkened room. The scent of the orange trees and of the flowers from the garden beyond, came in through the partly-opened window,

with the rich dry odour of a warm, African, summer morning.
(p. 3)

In this prelude the day-time pursuits of the young Rebekah on her South African farm are tenderly described, with a remarkable insight into the ways of a child's mind. There is little doubt that in the young Rebekah the young Olive Schreiner is once again being recreated.

Rebekah, early in womanhood, marries a conventional young man, and it seems that the course of her life will be smooth. In contrast, the younger of the sisters, Bertie, born at the opening of the book, soon reveals a proclivity for unhappiness. A less thoughtful, a more instinctive type physically than Rebekah, she is seduced when still young by her tutor, and in the cruel indulgence of a man's pleasure, we see how the seeds of Bertie's destruction are sown. When a suitor, the upright and highly 'moral' John-Ferdinand, presents himself, Bertie feels she must tell him the truth before she can accept him and realise happiness. In the following passage the author shows that at her best she was capable of an impressive psychological grip, as well as great tenderness:

'. . . I want to tell you something' [Bertie says]. '. . . Long ago I had a schoolmaster; his name was Percy Lawrie – I – I liked him – I liked him very much. – He was very kind to me. I liked him at first, then afterwards I hated him –' The hands she had now folded together in her lap were covered in the palms with a cold perspiration; ' – I did not know – he said he would be angry with me – I did not want him to be angry with me – I didn't want to – I didn't know, you see! – Oh, what shall I do!'

. . . John-Ferdinand looked down at her, white, motionless.

'He went away that day – I never saw him any more!'

John-Ferdinand leaned heavily on his arm on the rock above her, his face an ashen white. The scent of the crushed geraniums on which he stood seemed to rise up overpoweringly strong; and the only sound was the crying out of the

39

cicadas: they seemed glorying in the hot stillness of the
bush . . .

'Bertie, do you mean that you gave yourself to him?'
She nodded. (pp. 134–5)

This is too much for her morally over-fastidious suitor, and
he leaves her, although like a man of his word he expresses himself still willing to honour the marriage agreement if this is what
she wishes. Bertie, again bruised and bewildered, refuses his
offer. Her life has been set on its downward path. Constantly
now she is pursued by malicious whisperings, by each hurting
voice or glance thrust on her tragic journey, until eventually she
is found by Rebekah in a brothel, dying.

In indignant, passionate tones her creator condemns man's
inhumanity to man, his lack of charity and justice, precisely at
those times when these qualities are supremely required. She
points to the inadequacy of many of the conventions, and, indeed,
their frequent blindness to need.

Rebekah, the more thoughtful and articulate of the sisters, has
meanwhile found that her conventional husband (he calls her
the 'little woman' and treats her like an intellectually precocious
child), and the father of her four children, is consistently un-
faithful to her, Rebekah's coloured housemaid having become
his latest mistress. A seeker after probity in human relationships,
Rebekah will have nothing more to do with him sexually. When
the chance of love with another man presents itself she is constrained to refuse for the sake of her children. Her rejection of
happiness is not depicted as a preciously noble sacrifice – in this
portraiture of Rebekah the writer's indignation is leashed by the
artistic restraint of which she was sometimes capable.

There is considerable skill in the presentation of Rebekah.
Initially we see only the exterior of a small, apparently rather
cold, woman. Then in a long philosophical digression her pro-
pensity for abstract reasoning is explored – the abstractions are
given life by the desire for truth, for the undefinable, that underlies them. Her letter to her husband is an extended plea for love
and decency; the perspective is made to change again when we

see her as a patient, imaginative mother. The portrait, no doubt unorthodox in the way it is assembled, has, I think, the quality of 'completion'.

In the long interlude in which the story is interrupted to reveal the thoughts of Rebekah (and, therefore, of Olive Schreiner herself) what the writer implies in the action is given the force of direct and wider utterance – though it fails, perhaps, to have an artistically subtle consequence.

> . . . seek after truth. If anything I teach you be false, may you throw it from you, and pass on to higher and deeper knowledge than I ever had. If you are an artist, may no love of wealth or fame or admiration and no fear of blame or misunderstanding make you ever paint . . . an ideal or a picture of external life otherwise than as you see it; if you become a politician, may no success for your party or yourself or the seeming good of even your nation ever lead you to tamper with reality and play a diplomatic part. In all the difficulties which will arise in life, fling yourself down on the truth and cling to that as a drowning man in a stormy sea flings himself on to a plank and clings to it, knowing that, whether he sink or swim with it, it is the best he has. (p. 183)

This is, in part at least, a comment on the turbulences and storm of Olive Schreiner's own life, and why, in all her tempers, variations and wanderings, her struggles manage to communicate the sensation of rocklike trust.

Because she was trying to express something about the purposefulness of life and the courage of the human will, the writer in a long philosphical digression contests both the mechanistic and social aspects of Darwin's theory of the survival of the fittest. Who shall decide who is unfit? The creature with the longest claw and the greatest lust to destroy?

> . . . is it always the strongest fist and the fiercest heart which aids races or individuals to survive? Has not a great love lain behind those marvellous victories of which the world's history is full, . . . a love for an idea, for a race, for a land, which, by blotting out personal considerations, has given weakness the power to protect itself and survive? (p. 211)

In the course of the novel the writer covers a range of topics, including her recurrent theme of the relations between the sexes, relations where love and justice should be the conditioning elements; she attempts to delineate the truth and knowledge for which the human soul must always lust ('There is no small truth – all truth is great' (p. 181)); she reveals her sense of a divinity that penetrates every corner of life:

> Between spirit that beats within me and body through which it acts, between mind and matter, between man and beast, between beast and plant and plant and earth, between the life that has been and the life that is, I am able to see nowhere a sharp line of severance, but a great, pulsating, always interacting whole. So that at last it comes to be, that, when I hear my own heart beat, I actually hear in it nothing but one throb in that life which has been and is – in which we live and move and have our being and are continually sustained. (p. 181)

In hearing our own hearts beat, we achieve self-transcending forgetfulness, and hear the movement of the world. In such a way did the yearning temperament of Olive Schreiner seek the accord of her fine intelligence.

J. P. L. Snyman finds this philosophical digression wearying to the reader, and asserts that it has no place in fiction.[7] But surely the whole tradition of the novel supports innovation and adventure in technique? – Olive Schreiner, as in *An African Farm*, gives force, certainly interest, to what could seem a gross irrelevance. Vera Buchanan-Gould, with some justification, defends the interlude on the same grounds that she defends the Shakespearean soliloquy (p. 211).

Though fault may be found with the digressions, the characterisation, and the improbabilities (e.g. Rebekah's inordinately long letter to her husband), these defects, if such they are, do not overshadow the considerable perception behind the book. Re-

---

7. *The South African Novel in English (1880-1930)*, Potchefstroom University, 1952, pp. 16–8.

bekah's arguments to her children about racial injustice are skilfully treated, and bear favourable comparison with fashionable contemporary offerings on the topic. I do not, like Vera Buchanan-Gould, believe this book to be 'soul-shaking tragedy' (p. 208), but I do regard it as a notable, if incomplete, statement on the attitude of man to woman and therefore of man to man: it deals penetratingly with some of the problems of *Woman and Labour*, and should perhaps be read in conjuction with that book to attain a better appreciation of what Olive Schreiner sought in human relationships.

DREAM LIFE AND REAL LIFE

STORIES, DREAMS AND ALLEGORIES[1]

Olive Schreiner was our first notable English South African short story writer; today she would certainly not be regarded as our greatest. She had too many axes to grind, too many banners to wave, in what were, for her, days of artistic and political pioneering. She did not have the discipline or inclination to give complete attention to the form of her stories: to her the passion of the message was almost all important. Besides this, her contribution is too meagre to assure her enduring fame as a short story writer.

Yet much of what she saw in her restless wanderings she expressed tenderly and beautifully in the short story form. In 'Eighteen-Ninety-Nine', the Northern Transvaal, a part of South Africa the writer (according to her biographies) could not have known well, immediately comes to life. Intellectual London of 'The Buddhist Priest's Wife' is recreated with a similar conviction.

Only six short stories (apart from the two stories for children) survive – a very small total when we consider her not inconsiderable reputation in this field. Her best known story is 'Dream Life and Real Life', which has, I feel, been overrated. It is true that the writer captures the dream spirit, that misty borderline between imagination and reality, but, to use her own suggestion, it is not much more than a 'little' story, one of the first she 'made' as a young girl.[2] Her real achievement, in my opinion, is represented by 'Eighteen-Ninety-Nine' and 'The Buddhist Priest's Wife'.

In 'Eighteen-Ninety-Nine' Olive Schreiner fought another of

---

1. The bibliography indicates the contents of each of the volumes. Page references are to the appropriate volume.
2. Dedication, 1893 edition.

her notable battles in the cause of the Boer people, but what she achieves is much more than propaganda: her short story succeeds in acquiring many of the properties of the epic. It records the destinies of several Afrikaner generations with a compelling directness. There are no moral interludes, although the writer firmly makes her point against the opportunism of British politics at the turn of the century. The demands of theme and story are understandingly reconciled; ideas, events, setting, characterisation, achieve the indivisibility possible to a fine, fully-engaged imagination.

> It was a warm night: the stars shone down through the thick soft air of the Northern Transvaal into the dark earth, where a small daub-and-wattle house of two rooms lay among the long, grassy slopes. A light shone through the small window of the house, though it was past midnight. (p. 11)

The scene is presented, the right atmosphere is keyed, and the principal protagonist of the story is immediately introduced.

> Presently the upper half of the door opened and then the lower, and the tall figure of a woman stepped out into the darkness. (p. 11)

The actions of the woman constitute the central pillar of the story: husband, sons, grandson fall dead about her, but she stoically faces her stern God and an inscrutably relentless destiny. She fights tenaciously, vigorously for so long a time, that it is with a profound sense of shock that we are finally made to realise that she has become a very old woman:

> The younger woman raised her head slowly and looked up into her mother-in-law's face; and then, suddenly, she knew that her mother-in-law was an old, old woman. The little shrivelled face that looked down at her was hardly larger than a child's, the eyelids were half closed and the lips worked at the corners and the bones cut out through the skin in the temples. (p. 53)

Her family destroyed, the old woman works on in the lands until she dies in a British concentration camp. There is no sentimentality in the story – it is, simply, a record of human endurance and courage, fitted into a strong literary frame. The writer decisively fulfils an Aristotelian requirement: her story has a recognisable beginning, a coherent middle, and a conclusive end.

But apart from its considerable technical virtue, it is filled with the life and faith only a deeply committed temperament has the power of acquiring.

It has persistently been alleged that Olive Schreiner, despite her long polemical defences, had no inherent feeling for the Boer people, because her portraits of them in her creative writing are so consistently unfavourable. But this criticism cannot bear the scrutiny of 'Eighteen-Ninety-Nine', where we have a fully realised, a deeply sympathetic portrait of Boer life. There are, for example, the many quietly graphic descriptions of the old woman. We also have this portrait of the simple delights of Boer people:

> Outside the rain was pouring in torrents and you could hear the water rushing in the great dry sloot before the door. His grandmother, to amuse him, had sprung some dried mealies in the great black pot and sprinkled them with sugar, and now he sat on the stoof at her feet with a large lump of the sticky sweetmeat in his hand, watching the fire. (p. 32)

As usual, Olive's portraits of children are charmingly thoughtful:

> When she went to the lands to see how the Kaffirs were ploughing he would run at her side holding her dress; when they had gone a short way he would tug gently at it and say, 'Grandmother, tell me things!' (p. 29)

I regard 'Eighteen-Ninety-Nine' as a very fine story, indeed one of the best things Olive Schreiner ever wrote.

Though there is evidence[3] that the writer intended 'The Buddhist Priest's Wife' to be a full length novel, it is quite satisfying as it stands. Its focus is on one small room in a foggy London, and the conversation of two intelligent people who are not afraid to face the facts of their lives. It is hardly a short story at all. Yet the writer gives it interest and direction; as she so often does, she here

---

3. Cronwright-Schreiner's *Life of Olive Schreiner*, pp. 271 and 287.

projects her own personality into her characters – their conversation is her kind of conversation, their way of reasoning is her way. The mixture of creator and creation does not disturb, as it so often does in her novels. And despite its intellectual structure, simple pathos is not lacking in the story's conclusion.

In the woman depicted we recognise Olive Schreiner herself, an Olive Schreiner more attractively set down and more dispassionately seen than in any of her other writings. 'You are always going to get experience,' her visitor tells her, 'going to get everything, and you never do. You are always going to write when you know enough, and you are never satisfied that you do' (p. 67).

The two people, man and woman, air their views on life. 'There are only two things that are absolute realities,' the woman says, 'love and knowledge, and you can't escape them' (p. 67). 'No woman has the right to marry a man if she has to bend herself out of shape for him' (p. 71), she tells him later on, when they discuss marriage. These quotations may give the impression that the writer has once again taken to her feminist rostrum. But this would be an incorrect impression – the argument is skilfully worked into the fabric of the story. The whole thing is beautifully done.

Olive Schreiner projects something of herself into 'The Woman's Rose' and 'The Policy in Favour of Protection'; their effect is, however, far less happy than that of 'The Buddhist Priest's Wife', a similar type of story. 'On the Banks of a Full River' is rather too fragmentary for us to adjudge what its merits might or could have been.

The two children's stories 'The Wax Doll and the Stepmother' and 'The Adventures of Master Towser', are charmingly written: both are simple, and yet uncondescending. The first centres on the theme of love accepted; but the second again introduces rejected affection and ends on too disillusioned a note, one feels, for a children's story. The dog Towser has his creator's complaint: 'I want someone to love me,' he says urgently. 'I want to help somebody; I want to be of use' (p. 114).

DREAMS
STORIES, DREAMS AND ALLEGORIES

In *The Story of an African Farm* what Olive Schreiner felt she could not say adequately in the story itself she put into the fable of the hunter and the white bird of truth. What she felt she could not express clearly in her novels, in her political and social writings, and in the conduct of her own life, she found a voice for in her allegories, or, as she called them, her 'dreams'.

A good example of a message given an allegorical impact, and so transformed from the trite into the eloquent, is the very short 'Life's Gifts':

> I saw a woman sleeping. In her sleep she dreamt Life stood before her, and held in each hand a gift – in the one Love, in the other Freedom. And she said to the woman, 'Choose!'
>
> And the woman waited long: and she said, 'Freedom!'
>
> And Life said, 'Thou hast well chosen. If thou hadst said, "Love", I would have given thee that thou didst ask for; and I would have gone from thee, and returned to thee no more. Now, the day will come when I shall return. In that day I shall bear both gifts in one hand.'
>
> I heard the woman laugh in her sleep. (pp. 115–6)[1]

There is no fury and little passion in this: the statement is made, simply and unelaborately. One wonders how, amidst the turmoil and extravagance of her life, Olive Schreiner could write as economically as she does in 'Life's Gifts' – but perhaps life can indeed work by contraries, and a milieu of stir and pother can equip one for the task of seeing calmly and shaping firmly.

Olive Schreiner's dreams were not intended, however, as in-

---

1. Page references to *Dreams* are to the fourth edition (London, Unwin, 1892); to *Stories, Dreams and Allegories* they are to the first edition of 1923.

dulgences in tranquillity. Her portraits of Hell and Heaven in 'The Sunlight Lay Across My Bed' do little to lull the reader. In brilliantly sharp symbolic pictures she paints selfishness in the guise of the poisoners of fruit, and unscrupulous ambition in the diggers of pitfalls.

> I said to God, 'Why do they do it?'
>
> God said, 'Because each thinks that when his brother falls he will rise.' (p. 137)

This is an incisive statement of many enterprises in which personal ambition trafficks not recklessly (this could almost be forgivable), but calculatingly, in the deprivation of others.

In this dream God and the traveller pass together to a great house held up by marble pillars where handsome men and women feast on red wine – the wine is blood made from less fortunate human beings in a press concealed behind a vast curtain. Those at the banquet table call to God for 'more wine . . . more wine'. The revels grow wilder and wilder, the feasters become sick with what they have drunk. And then God leads the narrator to the ruins of previous feasting-houses which have destroyed themselves.

He then takes her to heaven, which consists of three parts, each successively higher than the other.[2] In the first heaven there is happiness, beauty and human companionship. In the second there is only labour, each labourer on the mountain-side discovering a small gem, his own finding and contribution, something he will add to the central crown they are creating.

> And the crown was wrought according to a marvellous pattern; one pattern ran through all, yet each part was different.
>
> I said to God, 'How does each man know where to set his stone, so that the pattern is worked out?'
>
> God said, 'Because in the light his forehead sheds each man sees faintly outlined that full crown.' . . .

---

2. In some ways Olive Schreiner's plans of heaven and hell recall Dante's far more complicated architecture in *The Divine Comedy*.

And I said, 'But what does each man gain by his working?' God [said], 'He sees his outline filled.'

I said, 'But those stones which are last set cover those which were first; and those will again be covered by those which come later.'

God said, 'They are covered, but not hid. The light is the light of all. Without the first, no last.' (pp. 171–2)

And the traveller has no longing to return to the first heaven, her eyes set on the crown.

This vision of the writer's that each man's donation to the sum of the good and the beautiful in life, that each man's contribution, however small, paves the way for other contributions, is also given expression in her most famous allegory, that of the hunter and the white bird of truth in *An African Farm*.

The hunter of truth has laboured slowly to the summit of the hill, giving his life to making the rough steps upwards. Death is near to him, and he cries:

Where I lie down worn out, other men will stand, young and fresh. By the steps that I have cut they will climb; by the stairs that I have built, they will mount . . . At the clumsy work they will laugh . . . But they will mount, and on *my* work; they will climb, and by *my* stair! They will find her, and through me! And no man liveth to himself, and no man dieth to himself. (pp. 49–50)

And what is to be found at the summit? The answer is given both in 'The Hunter', where the white bird passes overhead, and in 'The Sunlight Lay Across my Bed', where God takes the traveller to His third and highest heaven, a desolate mountain top. What comes to her on this peak is called 'music', which is here Olive Schreiner's word for truth.

God sends the traveller back to earth to make her own music there, according to the pattern of her gifts and seeking.

Each dream has the same spare, economical lines, and so giving shape to certain of Olive Schreiner's notions of truth. She herself attached great value to her allegories, feeling they expressed more cogently, more felicitously than anything else she had written, the longings of her inmost being – a being uncluttered at such moments by the political and social issues that all but consumed her. There certainly is in these dreams none of the blurring passion and the confusing digression that malformed much else that she wrote.

All the pieces so far discussed are contained in the volume simply called *Dreams*. Some of her further work was collected in a second volume entitled *Stories, Dreams and Allegories*, which, like their forerunners, are triumphs in spareness.

The most striking allegory in the second collection is 'Who Knocks at the Door?', one of her most forceful, and similar in some ways to 'The Sunlight Lay Across my Bed'. It was written in 1917, when the first World War was at its height, and it is a powerful dream picture of a civilisation destroying itself through greed and hate.

The dreamer wanders in a forest of impenetrable darkness, and comes on a mighty and beautiful building which resounds with laughter and from which light streams forth. She steals up to a window and looks into a beautiful banqueting hall in which a noble company, dressed in gorgeous robes and weighted with jewels, are feasting. The revellers shower jewels on one another, but with disquiet the watcher perceives that they have daggers at their sides.

Suddenly some of the company draw their daggers and a man and a woman fall dead; then the whole company rise up, fall on one another, until blood covers the floor and the windows are shattered. 'Stop it!' cries the watcher. 'Can you not see, you are destroying all?' But they pay no attention

> And in their madness I saw men drag down the great glittering lights that hung from the centre of the Hall, and fling the fragments at one another; and tear down the lighted torches that were fastened to the walls, and strike one another with them. And as the lights fell down on that seething mass that covered the floor, they set fire to the garments of the fallen and smoke began to rise. And outside the window where I stood came the stench of burning human flesh. (p. 152)

51

Flames creep up the walls. Then three knocks are distinctly heard and across the smoking hall the watcher sees a human face, looking in. She hurries away, and prays that the company knocking outside, if they rebuild the hall, will not have weapons at their sides, or drink wine that gives madness.

The author's favourite themes are again introduced in this volume – knowledge, love, truth. In 'The Two Paths'

> A soul met an angel and asked of him: 'By which path shall I reach heaven quickest – the path of knowledge or the path of love?' The angel looked at him wonderingly and said: 'Are not both paths one?' (p. 137)

To Olive Schreiner they were one, and that is why her perspective and penetration were at times so remarkably splendid.

THOUGHTS ON SOUTH AFRICA

Despite her high hopes for her authorship, there was always a compelling modesty in Olive Schreiner when she contemplated what she had achieved. In her letters she sometimes refers to her greatest novel as a 'little book', and she intended calling the present work simply *Stray Thoughts on South Africa* (e.g. *The Letters of Olive Schreiner*, pp. 12 & 200); that the thoughts are not random, but filled with a magnificent sense of consequence, now seems beyond gainsaying. 'It is simply what one South African at the end of the nineteenth century thought, and felt, with regard to his native land,' wrote Olive in her introduction, 'thought and felt with regard to its peoples, its problems and its scenery ... ' (p. 14).[1] But it is much more than this: it is the product of an exacting thinker, a polemical writing which more cogently, and graphically, expresses the character of South Africa and its people than any book before or since. It is in many ways quite the greatest book to come out of this country. Although the author and her husband confess to the book's scrappiness (like so much of her work it was incomplete at the time of her death) it is less fragmentary than one would be led to expect. The geographical features of the country, its fauna, and, most important, its inhabitants – Boer, British, Coloured and Native – are rendered by an extraordinary combination of penetration and generosity.

South Africa's natural features are recorded in the first chapter. The Boer (or Afrikaner, as he is now called) is exhaustively and sympathetically analysed in six chapters describing his way of life, his attitude to slavery, his wanderings, his womenfolk, his republics, and his character. To the Englishman of SouthAfrica

---

1. According to Cronwright-Schreiner's foreword to *Thoughts on South Africa* most of the chapters were written between 1890 and 1892; most of them were published as separate articles in various magazines between 1891 and 1900.

is devoted the long Chapter VIII, while the Cape Coloureds, Hottentots, Bushmen and Africans are ably dealt with, if less exhaustively, in the chapters 'The Problem of Slavery' and 'The Psychology of the Boer'. Finally, in the short section 'Our Waste Land in Mashonaland' the writer pleads, before the Kruger or the Wanki National Parks were realised, for the founding of a great reserve for the preservation of the animal life of Southern Africa·

Olive Schreiner had a profound admiration and love for the South African Boer (although her attitude was not completely uncritical). What she admired most in him was his simplicity in an age of materialism, his retention of personal values in an age when stock values were at a premium. 'He still believes there are things money cannot buy,' she writes, 'that a man may have three millions of money in syndicate shares, and hold command over the labour of ten thousand workers, and yet be no better than he who goes out every morning in his leather trousers to tend his own sheep' (p. 98). She was troubled by the thought that these values might be offered up, even by the Boer, for flashier things. In an impassioned plea she asks the Boer people not to exchange their simple, yet rich lives for something apparently more attractive, but which would ultimately prove shallow and ephemeral:

Hold fast, Tante! Hold fast, Oom! You have much to lose. Be careful how you exchange it. Cling to your old manners, your old faiths, your free, strong lives, till you know what you are bartering them for. (p. 269)

The writer's descriptions of Boer family life are both succinct and graphic, and her style at such times takes on a becoming simplicity. The tool bends with perfect instinct to shape its material, and we are reminded at such times that Olive Schreiner could be a consummate artist. The descriptions on pages 162–190 and 388–392 are invaluable portraits of Boer life, Boer life as the writer knew it in the latter half of the nineteenth century.

In the chapter on the psychology of the Boer the specific charges brought against the Boer people are listed, and each is exhaustively refuted: that he was a coward and could not fight

('It has been said, though it will probably never be said again by any person who knows what courage is . . .' (p. 249) – she explains that this idea may have arisen because the Boer fought not for the love of conflict but out of grim necessity); that he was conservative; that he was priest-ridden; that he was bigoted and ntolerant in religious matters; that he was superstitious about his faith, and allowed it to dominate every concern of his life; that his dealings with the African native were unjust.

The backbone of the Boer's way of life was his simple Taal: '. . . it has,' she writes, 'been the prime conditioning element in his life . . .' The other great conditioning element was his unquestioning love of this country and his understanding of its unique geographical spirit.

> . . . these men, and the women who bore them, possessed South Africa as no white man has ever possessed it, and as no white man ever will, save it be here and there a stray poet or artist. They possessed it as the wild beasts and the savages whom they dispossessed had possessed it; they grew out of it; it shaped their lives and conditioned their individuality. They owed nothing to the men of the country, and everything to the inanimate nature about them! (p. 160)

The Boer, as she saw him, did not pause to meditate this love; it simply became part of his being.

The life he led made his view of things refreshingly unclouded: '. . . when upon the untaxed brain, through the untaxed nerves of sense, every sight and sound trace themselves with delicious clearness and merely to live and hear the flies hum – is a pleasure' (p. 185). This untrammelled way of life was qualifying the Boer to participate in all the higher duties of a civilised state; the unceasing pressures of city life had debilitated the intellect and body of other men, but 'in the peaceful silences of the veld the Boer's nerve and brain have probably reposed and recuperated; therefore the descendant to-day, thrown suddenly into the hurrying stream of modern life, appears in it with the sound nerves and couched-up energy of generations; though whether he will retain these under modern conditions is to be seen' (p. 222). Most of our great statesmen and judges have, as if to give emphasis to the writer's argument, been of Boer descent. The warning of the final sentence is, however, unmistakable.

In a short historical resumé she brilliantly adumbrates the causes of the Great Trek. She deals with the Boer's peripatetic instinct with considerable perception, and makes of that instinct something clearly admirable; indeed its proportion is almost epic:

> With a constant tendency to go northward and north-east these men moved slowly on; visiting for the first time plain after plain in the karoo and grass-veld, and piloting their huge canvas-sailed wagons across the infinite expanses of sand and rock, as their sailor forefathers a few generations earlier had piloted their ships across the sea.
>
> In many cases for generations this wandering life was continued. Men were born, grew up, grew old, and died, who knew no home but the ox-wagon, and had no conception of human life but as a perpetual moving onward. (p. 158)

In *Woman and Labour* Olive Schreiner emerged as a redoubtable evangelist in the feminist cause, devoting much of her most impassioned writing to pleading for a greater share for women in the labour of the world. She had no time for what she described as the 'parasite female', who lived a life of idleness and luxury, depending for her well-being on the labour of others. The Boer woman, the writer felt, had an important lesson to teach womankind – 'she takes an equally large and valuable share in the common work of life' (p. 200). She addresses the Boer woman as follows: '. . . do not decay from your ancient simplicity of living and toiling before the time is ripe and you can move forward to new labours' (p. 271). Unelaborate the Boer's work might be, but the writer held the view that all genuine labour was ennobling, and the women produced by it far more enduring than those European women reclining in their drawing rooms 'so frequently mentally vacuous and feeble, in whom the passive enjoyment of ease has taken the place of all strenuous systematic exertion . . .' (p. 203). Olive Schreiner was a pioneer of the feminist movement, and wrote before the franchise and common opportunity had become the plea of so many European women.

In the Englishman of South Africa she saw a teasing Jekyll and Hyde: on the one hand, a pleader for individual freedom and dignity; on the other, a land-grabbing materialist and a mouther of cant. Although to a large extent the unpleasant side of the Englishman in this country had been seen, the writer insisted that there was another side, and that in many walks of life the Englishman had distinguished himself all the world over; for example, as missionary and statesman he had contributed substantially to the raising of human standards.

When his representatives abroad debased themselves there was reason for bitterness, for she cherished a dream for the English people as a great unifying force in the world. The Englishman was especially equipped for this role, she argued, because – though England may not have produced the greatest artists, musicians and civil governments – she had held before her more than any other nation the banner, 'the tradition and fact of personal freedom' (p. 340). On the whole 'we [she here identifies herself with the English] love liberty so dearly that we would not willingly inflict an injustice or a wrong on another, and we respect the freedom of others while we venerate our own' (p. 343). England's contribution to the cause of human freedom was distinctive and dynamic, in its constant affirmation

> that man as man is a great and important thing, that the right to himself and his existence is the incontestable property of all men; and above all the conviction that not only *we* have a right and are bound to preserve it for ourselves, but that where we come into contact with others *we are bound to implant it or preserve it in them*. It is a profound faith, not in the equal talent, virtues, and abilities of men, but in the equal right of the poorest, most feeble, most ignorant, to his own freedom and to a perfect equality of treatment. (p. 351)

In this country the role of the Englishman had often been one of hypocrite; he had associated himself with several shabby enterprises while canting about their beneficence. But, according to

57

the commentator, he had only indulged in this hypocrisy because of the shame he felt, because ultimately, even in the lowest representatives of his nation, he had been aware of the dignity of all human life: 'We have meant to aid and raise them, to put them on an equality with ourselves, and the thought they were being crushed or murdered would be a blow to the most earnest sensibilities of our natures' (p. 346). When Olive Schreiner wrote this chapter she saw a chance for England to play a great unifying role in South Africa, but in 1900 after the debacle of the Chartered Company, the Jameson Raid, and the Boer War, she decided abruptly: 'that she [England] has committed suicide in South Africa is a matter for no doubt' (p. 381).

According to Olive Schreiner, the most marked result of slavery in this country was the bringing into existence of the Cape Coloured people, or, as the writer still called them, the Half-castes. The white people of South Africa could not afford to turn their eyes away, for they had helped create the Half-caste. This is expressed with characteristic vigour: 'He is here, our own; we have made him; we cannot wash our hands of him . . . The Half-caste is our own open, self-inflicted wound . . .' (p. 141); 'An analysis of the condition of the Half-caste brings home to us, as nothing else can do, our own racial responsibility towards him' (p. 140). Because of our responsibility, it was incumbent on us to contribute to the improvement of his position: the Cape Coloured, as she pointed out, was an insecure person, the result largely of illicit sexual relations; in this social amorphousness he was totally unlike the African whose life was firmly rooted in strong tribal traditions.

For the African she pleads: do not destroy the structure of his society until there is something better to put in its place. 'It may be easy to break down and demoralise our great, and at present noble, Bantu races; but it may be very hard ever to build them up again' (p. 317). And, ultimately, what was their destiny to be? If someone should ask her (and, by implication, those for whom she speaks) 'Well, but what do you intend this country to be, a black man's country or a white?', she tells us that she would reply, 'we intend nothing. If the black man cannot labour or bear the strain and stress of complex civilised life, he will pass away. We need not degrade and injure ourself by killing him; if *we* cannot work here, then in time, wholly or in part, the white man will pass away . . .' (p. 360); and 'if it be suggested to us that the Natives of the land are ignorant, we have the reply to make that we are here to teach them all we know if they will learn – if they will not, they must fall' (p. 361). And 'if it be asked whether we think them our equals, we would reply: Certainly in love of happiness and their own lives – perhaps not in some other directions; but we are here to endeavour to raise them as far as it is possible . . .' (p. 361). We should learn courageously to accept their inevitable advance. Morally and intellectually what became of them was a matter of vital concern to us; we and 'our descendants have got to sail with the African native permanently in the same ship across the sea of time . . .' (p. 313).

When she wrote these chapters[2] the African was almost entirely in a position of domestic servitude, and the problem of black and white relationships in the field of labour was not yet fully apparent; 'but in fifty years' time,' she predicted, 'this harmonising of black and white men in the higher walks of life will probably form a great part of the South African problem' (p. 309). Her attitude was that the African would ultimately have to enter our civilisation, and that all European people in this country would have to co-operate in effecting this; 'if [South Africa's] native races are to be transformed from dumb brooding enemies, borne within her bosom, to citizens who shall be the joy and strength of her commonwealth, it will not be through the action of Dutchmen or Englishmen alone; but of brave souls irrespective of all descent . . . hand in hand' (p. 320). 'He may grasp,' she believed, 'what is great in our civilisation along with its evils and may yet become the most valuable element and the ablest defender of a social organisation in which he has much at stake' (p. 319).

2. See previous note.

Olive Schreiner's views on the impossibility of apartheid are interesting (the separatist idea is certainly more than a few decades old). Total separation was, to her, not even thinkable. 'The blending has now gone too far. There is hardly a civilised roof in South Africa that covers people of only one nation; in our households, in our families, in our very persons we are mingled' (p. 59). The initiative was frighteningly in our hands. She reminds us that 'rank confers obligation'; 'deal with thy fellow man as, wert thou in his place, thou wouldst have him deal with thee' (pp. 317–8).

Throughout the book the writer shows her opposition to the materialism which was fast becoming the obsession of the nineteenth century (and which from that time has grown into its present-day dominion). Time and again she tells the Boer that we have need of his simplicity and clear-mindedness to face 'civilisation with its colossal evils, and its infinite beneficial possibilities . . .' (p. 151). As we have seen, what she particularly admired in him was his indifference to the mere trappings of the age:

> In the whirl and din of our material advancement, in the fierce struggle for external gains and progress, there is a side of life we have well nigh forgotten, and the Boer on his solitary South African plains has saved up a tradition we have forgotten and for need of which we may yet die . . .
>
> While we bring to the Boer the doctrine of a higher humanity, the external literary culture which enlarges the power of the man, he has his own lessons for us. While we have set gold on a pedestal and dance till we are drunk around it like the Israelites about their calf, the Boer, nurtured in his primitive solitude, still knows there are things our god cannot give us, and that material luxury and wealth are not the beginning and end of life, that the man is not greater because his name can stir three millions in the bank, that the cut of a coat is an accident, and that a man sees God as nearly face to face from the front box of his wagon as from the steps of a queen's palace
>
> . . . a train is better than an ox-wagon only when it carries

better men; rapid movement is an advantage only when we move towards beauty and truth . . . The size of our houses and the labour of a thousand weary hands upon our walls do not necessarily give us the happiness you would think. (pp. 328–9)

Though we can get other people to do our dirty work for us, and then proceed to overlook its existence, 'it may be questioned whether what we gain in refinement we have not lost in sincerity' (p. 158).

She questions the values of a materialistic world:

Though we increase endlessly the complexity of our material possessions and our desires, does the human creature who desires and possesses necessarily expand with them? And the answer which comes back to us when we deeply consider this question is: No. (p. 260)

The human spirit may well become smaller and tighter, closed in by the Thou-shalts and Thou-shalt-nots of a system based so strongly on material achievement. For though

we rush from end to end of the earth with the speed of lightning, . . . we love it no better than men who lived in their valley and went no further than their feet would carry them: we put the whole world under contribution to supply our physical needs, but the breath of life is no sweeter to us than to our forefathers whom the products of one land could satisfy. (p. 261)

She reminds us that 'the world's literature has been produced in simplicity and in poverty, and often in suffering . . .' (p. 265). Without belief in the spiritual quality of things life has little significance: 'There is perhaps no life quite worth living without a living religion, under whatever name or form it may be concealed, vivifying and strengthening it' (p. 285).

The quality of her keen, responsive mind is perhaps best seen in her prophecies. This book has many prophecies, and most of them have been realised. For example, in 1900 she predicted the great World War of 1914–1918 (p. 378); in 1901 she stated that

Russia would be one of 'the mighty modifying forces of the future' (p. 22); and also in 1901 she foresaw that the admixture of the different races of the earth, European and Asian and African, would 'be the world's question' (p. 385). To her there was nothing particularly wonderful in the fact that she was able to come to these conclusions (p. 61): she drew on the knowledge she had accumulated in her somewhat catholic studies, and, capable as she was of exceptionally steady thinking, proceeded to give logic to her observations. That a person who was not a scientist should write the following, and in the nineteenth century, is, however, impressive: 'The chemical discovery made to-day by a man of science in his laboratory and recorded in the pages of the scientific journal, is modifying the work in a thousand other laboratories throughout Europe before the end of the week' (p. 94).

In some ways Olive Schreiner may be considered one of the spiritual founders of the South African nation, for even in the divided South Africa of the eighteen-nineties she saw the country as an entity; she saw and believed in its eventual unity, though she pleaded that that unity should be realised gradually and spontaneously in order to make it completely secure; she argued that any attempt to weld it together artificially by force would result in endless difficulties and recurring divisions between the peoples of which the nation would be composed. '... if to-morrow,' she wrote, 'it [union] were effected by external force, the blow at our internal and vital unity would be almost irrecoverable' (p. 325). She pleaded that 'the nation can and must wait for true unity, which can only come as the result of internal growth and the union of its atoms . . . A nation grows, but it cannot be manufactured' (p. 324). Though she passionately desired eventual union it was not to be bought at the cost of one of the constituent units surrendering to the other: '. . . there is a price too high even for union, the price of the integrity of the parties composing it' (p. 326).

Although South Africa included many different races she did not regard this as a factor which would militate against union, because the composition of the then independent states – the

Cape Colony, Natal, the Transvaal, and the Orange Free State –
each consisted of this admixture of almost identical racial elements. Indeed the bond which was or would grow between the
states owed much to the different races of which each consisted:

> Wherever a Dutchman, an Englishman, a Jew, and a native
> are superimposed, there is that common South African con-
> dition through which no dividing line can be drawn. The
> only form of organisation which can be healthily or naturally
> assumed by us is one which takes cognisance of this universal
> condition. (p. 61)

She would not like to see the disappearance of any one of the
South African races in effecting this union – variety made it
attractive: 'Each race has its virtues and the deficiencies which
are complemental to its virtues, and the loss of any one race would
be to me the falling of a star from the human galaxy' (p. 21).
South Africa had the great and stimulating 'twentieth-century
problem of the mixture and government of mixed peoples' (p. 366)
on which posterity would not fail to deliver judgement – but, and
the warning is once again unmistakable, 'if the South Africa of
the future is to remain eaten internally by race hatreds, a film
of culture and intelligence spread over seething masses of ignorance and brutality, inter-support and union being wholly
lacking; then, though it may be our misfortune rather than our
fault, our doom is sealed; our place will be wanting among the
great, free nations of earth' (pp. 63–4).

It is perhaps important to emphasise how deeply Olive Schreiner loved South Africa. Her judgements were not simply the products of a remote observer, but came from a passionate partici-
pant – although at the same time she had the command of intellect that would allow her to see issues clearly. Her vision, singularly unclouded by delusions, was yet the result of a deep love.
For this reason it has abiding value for us: '. . . . if it may be said,'
she writes, 'that no man understands a thing till he has coldly
criticised it, it may also be said that no man knows a thing till he
has loved it' (pp. 29–30). To know our problems, you must know
our country – its land, its peoples, its storms, its wealth, its poverty.

Possibly few people have known South Africa better, with the emotions and the intellect, than Olive Schreiner.

In *Thoughts on South Africa* we have numerous loving descriptions of the natural bounty of this sub-continent. In her introductory chapter the writer roves the country, describing its physical features, dwelling on those she loves and knows best. As we realise from *An African Farm* it was the Karoo, in particular, that effected an intense love. In *Thoughts on South Africa* there are several descriptions that bear comparison with those of the more famous book:

> In the spring, in those years when rain has fallen, for two months the Karoo is a flower garden. As far as the eye can reach, stretch blots of white and yellow and purple fig flowers; every foot of Karoo sand is broken open by small flowering lilies and waxflowers . . .
>
> Nor less wonderful is the Karoo at night, when the Milky Way forms a white band across the sky; and you stand alone outside and see the velvety blue-black vault rising slowly on one side of the horizon and sinking on the other; and the silence is so intense you seem almost to hear the stars move. Nor is it less wonderful on moonlight nights, when you sit alone on a kopje; and the moon has arisen and the light is pouring over the plain; then even the stones are beautiful; and what you have believed of human love and fellowship – and never grasped – seems all possible to you. (pp. 38–41)

The following passage seems to acquire the spirit of the land itself, for it vividly evokes what the writer saw, felt, and loved:

> In the Western Province the coast belt consists of chains of huge mountains forming a network over a tract of country some hundreds of miles in extent . . . In the still, peaceful valleys at the feet of these mountains are running streams; in the spring the African heath covers them with red, pink and white bells, and the small wine-farms dot the sides of the valleys with their white houses and green fields, dwarfed under the high, bare mountains. Here and there are little towns and villages, built as only the old Dutch-Huguenots

64

knew how to build, the long, straight streets lined with trees on either hand, and streams of water running down them; and the old thatch-roofed, gabled, white-washed, green-shuttered houses standing back, with their stone stoeps, under the deep shade of the trees, and with their vineyards and orchards behind them. (pp. 30–1)

Her restless spirit, stifled by asthma and social restriction, found freedom in the huge spaces of South Africa. It is clear that in the fibre of her being she was a South African:

... there is a certain colossal plenitude, a certain large freedom in all its natural proportions, which is truly characteristic of South Africa. If Nature here wishes to make a mountain, she runs a range for five hundred miles; if a plain, she levels eighty; if a rock, she tilts five thousand feet of strata on end; our skies are higher and more intensely blue; our waves larger than others; our rivers fiercer. There is nothing measured, small nor petty in South Africa. (p. 50)

And one of her principal pleas is: let our people, to match this landscape, not be measured or petty, but responsive and generous, and worship only before the throne of the true and the beautiful.

Throughout this work one is aware of Olive Schreiner as a considerable thinker, a magnanimous human being, a great lover of life in its variety of forms; but with all these qualities she would have failed to bring home her message had she not been a highly gifted writer. Time and again we are aware of the style she commands and the expressive power on which she draws either to give vigour to her argument, or to evoke the spirit of what she describes. If she does sometimes use terms that seem stiff and curious, such as 'acceptation' and 'exemplification', they, too, seem often to be transmuted into eminently suitable words because of the oratorical conviction with which they are used.

None of the writer's conclusions are flashy. Though the book is full of theories, most of them are singularly profound. Olive Schreiner – contrary to the impact of the existing biographies, or even of her letters – was a vigorous thinker. The book is a monument to the range of her powers as an observer and commentator.

AN ENGLISH SOUTH AFRICAN'S VIEW OF THE SITUATION

An English South African's View of the Situation was one of Olive Schreiner's propaganda pieces. Her husband, in his *Life of Olive Schreiner*, relates how she wrote and produced this pamphlet at tremendous speed as her contribution in 1899 towards averting the impending disaster of an Anglo-Boer war. As propaganda it is clear-thoughted and admirable, but as literature it is far below most of her other work and repeats many of the points made so well in *Thoughts on South Africa*. There are some examples of over-writing: 'Has our race in Africa and our race in England interests so diverse that any calamity so cataclysmic can fall upon us as war!' (p. 76). Even in a tract such as this, the cry of the soapbox orator is at times painfully obvious. The following is the type of statement to which Olive Schreiner does not often succumb: '. . . it will assuredly be clear to all impartial and truth-loving minds . . .' (p. 62).

The real interest for us of *An English South African's View of the Situation* is not as literature (it was never intended as such, although Olive Schreiner was always on her guard against poor writing), or as propaganda (its impact was intended for its own time and can, possibly, be little felt in ours). The tract is important for the woman it reveals.

Although this was an urgent cry against a threatening war, the pamphleteer was able dispassionately to see the issues in question, and what she wrote becomes therefore a tribute to the clarity of a mind under stress. Her elucidation of the differences between the numerically small South African Republic (the Transvaal) and its large Uitlander settlement at Johannesburg is particularly valuable. Her stand on behalf of both the Repub-

66

lics was not merely a blind ardency, but an honest deliberation of the rights and wrongs of the cause she championed.

Whatever the shortcomings of her medium as literature, her sweeping challenge in this pamphlet must perhaps be amongst the finest writing of its type. She concedes that England with her tremendous resources of manpower, money and armaments would probably be able easily to overrun the Republics (this task proved to be much more difficult than was expected), but reminds England that 'the hour of external success may be the hour of irrevocable failure . . .' (p. 82). She cries to the British soldier: '. . . there are no laurels for you here!' (p. 80), and sees behind the splendid façade of the war-machine, the old misty figure of greed. South Africa, to most of the people interested in propagating a war, is 'a hunting ground . . . , a field for extracting wealth . . .' (p. 56). Several times she insists that love, not war, will tie the bonds of South Africa and England, will blend the races of South Africa into 'a great mutual people' (p. 78) and obliterate the lines of distinction between the English and Afrikaans speaking sections of the population (p. 29).

That her attempt to avert war failed has become irrelevant. The motives behind the attempt remain important.

CLOSER UNION

In 1908 Olive Schreiner was asked by the editor of *The Transvaal Leader* to give her views on the possible union of the states of South Africa. With her characteristic thoroughness on public and national issues, she attacked this task, and in her article we have a well directed, often brilliant, summation of what she considered the main concerns of such a union to be. This article is particularly interesting in that it is more illuminating than any of her other writings about her attitude to the 'Coloured Question'.

'I am of opinion,' she states unequivocally, 'that where the Federal franchise is concerned, no distinction of race or colour should be made between South Africans. All persons born in the country or permanently resident here should be one in the eye of the State . . . South Africa must be a free man's country . . . I believe that an attempt to base our national life on distinctions of race and colour, as such will, after the lapse of many years, prove fatal to us' (pp. 7–8).[3]

She gives particular attention to the Native Question[4] because she held it 'to be the root question in South Africa; and as is our wisdom in dealing with it, so will be our future' (pp. 23–4). She indicates, too, that the overwhelming presence of the Native people does not only represent a 'problem' in this country, but constitutes a great economic advantage. 'They are the makers of our wealth, the great basic rock on which our State is founded – our vast labouring class' (p. 25). She was in favour of an educational test for all those desiring the franchise; Natives would not automatically be debarred, nor would all white persons automatically be eligible. She set great store by the franchise and the standard of its participants.

It was on the Coloured Question that South Africa had a peculiar contribution to make to progress. The writer predicted that South Africa would be one of the first testing grounds of the world for the meeting of various races, and it was on the solution she found to this problem that her international reputation would rest. 'On our power to solve it regally and heroically,' she wrote, 'depends our greatness' (p. 26). South Africa had an important role to play in the 'interaction of distinct human varieties on the largest and most beneficent lines, making for the development of humanity as a whole, and carried out in a manner consonant with modern ideals and modern social wants' (p. 26). She added significantly: 'It will not always be the European who forms the upper layer . . .' (p. 26).

The whole question represented a magnificent challenge to

3. Page references are to the (undated) edition published in Cape Town by The Constitutional Reform Association.

4. I am using the word then current for African or Bantu, because Olive Schreiner herself used it extensively in the article.

European intelligence, and it was a most wonderful opportunity to bind the black races to us, not through servility and fear, but 'through their sense of justice and gratitude . . .' (p. 28). A solution was an urgent necessity, or 'are we', asked the writer, 'to spend all our national existence with a large, dark shadow looming always in the background – a shadow-which-we-fear?' (p. 30). She foresaw clear-sightedly what the issue would be, and this is the question we have to face today, with the solution apparently growing more and more elusive as we let slip our opportunities to conciliate our dark races. The shadow ever more quickly grows larger and darker.

The writer also expressed her views on other aspects of a possible union. She was in favour of federation as opposed to a close union, because she felt that small, independent states, loosely bonded together, allowed greater individual freedom and worked more effectively than the dehumanising uniformity of a great national unit. A federation of small self-governing states would also work against the possibility of a dictatorship ever being established. In considering the claims of the various provinces she emphasised that whatever form of union was entered into, sacrifices would have to be made. On the question of the capital of the new state, she felt that a completely new federal centre should be established. Such a capital would build up its own associations of federal unity. In putting forward this proposal she no doubt had the example of Washington in the United States in mind.

She was, however, adamantly opposed to hurrying into an artificial form of union, a union forced without complete preparation, on the participating South African states. It would be like 'building sand-houses' (p. 19), to be swept away by the tide of some great event because its foundations had not been prepared with sufficient care. '. . . a nation cannot be manufactured,' she warns us, as she did in *Thoughts on South Africa*, '. . . it exists and grows from its own roots . . .' (p. 21). That a large nation was automatically stronger than a small nation she regarded as nonsense, asking the question whether a big feeble man of 350 pounds was automatically more healthy and capable than an active man of 120.

She felt that at such a time, when union was becoming of paramount interest, a great leader was required to help in the spontaneous unification of the people: as she put it – 'the hearts of great men unite peoples' (p. 36).

Closer Union is a significant document: it is clear-sighted, well-reasoned, humane, idealistic, realistic, truthful, generous; indeed a most important piece of literature in helping us define what we wish to make of our country. As I have said before, Olive Schreiner was an extremely able writer on political and humanitarian matters, and *Closer Union* is one of the finest of her political texts.

OTHER POLITICAL WRITINGS

Olive Schreiner could be regarded as a fairly persistent commentator on immediate contemporary issues, most of what she wrote being in the form of addresses to be read either by herself or a deputy. Yet though such statements reveal the aliveness of her mind, they are not up to the standard of those works she clearly intended for wide publication. The cry is vehement, the plea eloquent, and the argument thoughtful, but outside their own time they cannot have great interest or impact for those who are concerned with her status as writer and thinker. In *A Letter on the Jew*, which was written to coincide with a campaign against a wave of anti-semitic feeling which was then sweeping the Cape, she pleads for justice and consideration for a race and its traditions, for a people who have contributed so much to civilisation. In *The Political Situation*, written jointly with her husband, and delivered by Cronwright-Schreiner at a meeting held in 1895 in Kimberley, the stronghold of Rhodes, she forcefully attacked the corruptions of the Rhodes party. She also delivered herself of a strong defence of liberalism and personal integrity, and proposed that a Progressive Liberal Party should be formed in the Cape to combat retrogressive and insincere political developments, the tendency as she put it of 'playing [politics] to make points' (p. 146). Her other addresses were mainly in defence of the woman's movement or the Boers, or pleas against war.

Although at times, as in *The Dawn of Civilisation*, Olive Schreiner felt her pleas to be materially ineffectual – that she was battering in vain against bias and ignorance – she yet continued her fight. Apart from meeting the needs of her own integrity, she felt that her efforts would not be entirely wasted, somewhere there were people who cherished ideals like her own. 'You . . . are a part of the great Universe,' she wrote in *The Dawn of Civilisation*, 'what you strive for something strives for; *and nothing in the Universe is quite alone;* you are moving on towards something' (*Stories, Dreams and Allegories*, 1924 edition, p. 170).

WOMAN AND LABOUR

Olive Schreiner was probably in her teens when, in a somewhat ironical tone, she wrote the following in *Undine*: 'Is not all work, if it be earnestly done, noble and ennobling?' (p. 199). This idea was to form the basis of her highly earnest plea in *Woman and Labour*: do not take away from woman the nobility of work or she will degenerate into a worthless parasite female. She was persistently to preach feminism, a little crudely in novels such as *The Story of an African Farm* and in *From Man to Man* – in *Woman and Labour*, however, her polemic attains her maturest expression, even, possibly, resounding eloquence.[1]

Her plea is clearly made in the opening paragraph of the book: 'Give us labour and the training which fits for labour!' (p. 33). In the first three chapters she examines the incidence of the parasite female: if not given work, or if not made fit for it, someone who will gradually pull her race down with her into a state of vacuity and degeneration. In great sweeping sentences the writer traces the development of man and woman from the earliest times when they wandered over the earth together. In a primitive world woman shared in the labour of man: if he was the protector and fighter, she was the creator of the race and its sustainer. When their nomadic existence came to an end, their labour was still divided, for he was the hunter, and she the tiller of fields. But gradually, as the necessity for fighting and hunting diminished, man began to absorb the functions of woman, and her area of labour became more and more circumscribed – it included not much more than the preparation of food and the spinning and

1. The voguish 'Women's Lib' of the nineteen sixties and seventies has a great deal to learn, I think, from 'Victorian' commentators such as Olive Schreiner. It is the continuation of a movement that owed much to those who prepared the ground by the quality of their thinking; it is by no means a wildly original phenomenon.

weaving of cloth. Then came mechanical power, and what had been human muscular effort began to reassemble itself as intellectual work. New, wide fields of labour opened before man, but woman's means of endeavour, now to a large extent replaced by machinery, continued contracting and disappearing, until woman could no longer even claim to be the educator of her children, that function being given into the hands of a specialist worker. With the drop in child mortality, woman's constant services in the field of child-bearing were no longer required, and many unmarried women, by the development of our social code, were compelled to go childless. Women did not demand the return of the old conditions, but only 'that in this new world we also shall have our share of honoured and socially useful human toil, our full half of the labour of the Children of Woman' (p. 68).

It was imperative that women find new fields of labour; otherwise they would fall to the evil of sex-parasitism, something which, if allowed to continue unchecked, would eventually enervate the human race. That from weak and parasitic mothers only weak and enervated children would develop, was one of the burdens of the writer's argument. In all those states, such as Greece and Rome, where the female parasite had appeared in the dominant class, the advent of internal weakening and decline had been signalled, until these once great world states were destroyed by virile surrounding tribes.

The parasite female developed in the upper classes of those ancient states where slave labour was extensively employed. In the modern world the place of slave labour had been taken by machinery. This made our problem even graver. For in those ancient states, the parasite female was confined mainly to one class: a parasitic female upper class usually meant a labouring slave class, which included women. But with the advent of the machine, the parasite female was penetrating to all social strata. The coming half-century, the writer warns us, would be 'a time of peculiar strain, as mankind seeks rapidly to adjust moral ideals and social relationships and the general ordering of life to the new and continually unfolding material conditions' (p. 124).

The writer admits that in the ranks of militant feminism there had undoubtedly been individual failures, disappointing examples of narrow self-interest. Yet on the whole woman was working not only for her own promotion in the field of labour but in answer to a larger impersonal obligation – the status of humankind. For 'without the reaction of interevolution between sexes, there can be no real and permanent human advance' (p. 132):

> Our woman's movement resembles strongly . . . the gigantic religious and intellectual movement which for centuries convulsed the life of Europe; and had, as its ultimate outcome, the final emancipation of the human intellect and the freedom of the human spirit. (p. 136)

In subsequent chapters it is argued that there was no proof that woman was fitted mentally only for certain restricted fields of intellectual activity; and that man was not so much opposed to the principle that woman should labour, but that she should draw remuneration to rival his or enter fields which he had reserved as his own. There should be no artificial restrictions, the writer argued, for she believed that 'every individual unit humanity contains, irrespective of race, sex, or type, should find exactly that field of labour which may most contribute to its development, happiness, and health, and in which its peculiar faculties and gifts shall be most effectively and beneficially exerted for its fellows' (p. 216).

She proceeds to deal with those apparently telling objections to the improvement of woman's status as a worker. These include the hoary one that if women enter modern fields of labour they will become unfeminine and tend to set minor store by sexual responsiveness. 'There is absolutely no ground,' the writer contends, 'for the assumption that increased intelligence and intellectual power diminishes sexual emotion in the human creature of either sex' (p. 232). In fact increased intelligence and sensitivity tend to develop rather than diminish sexual passion. The emergence of women in professions also tends to diminish the evil of prostitution, and of 'all forced sexual relationships based, not on the spontaneous affection of the woman for the man, but on the necessitous acceptance by woman of material good in exchange for the exercise of her sexual functions . . .' (p. 245). The Woman's Movement should be regarded as the volition 'of the sexes towards each other, a movement towards common occupations, common interests, common ideals, and towards an emotional sympathy between the sexes more deeply founded and more indestructible than any the world has yet seen' (p. 259). The age of the vacuous woman partner, someone who is unable to take any part in her husband's intellectual life, must pass. 'A certain mental camaraderie and community of impersonal interests is imperative in conjugal life in addition to a purely sexual relation, if the union is to remain a living and always growing reality' (p. 279). Some of the most enduring of marriages have come into being where a common labour and common ideals have been the basis.

Olive Schreiner ends her book with an example of the impressive oratory she seemed so instinctively to have at her command:

> Always in our dreams we hear the turn of the key that shall close the door of the last brothel; the clink of the last coin that pays for the body and soul of a woman; the falling of the last wall that encloses artificially the activity of woman and divides her from man; always we picture the love of the sexes, as, once a dull, slow, creeping worm; then a torpid, earthy chrysalis; at last the full-winged insect, glorious in the sunshine of the future. (p. 281)

THE LETTERS OF OLIVE SCHREINER 1876–1920
(edited by her husband, S. C. Cronwright-Schreiner)

Unlike many notable figures of literature, Olive Schreiner did not intend her letters for publication. In fact, the prospect of some of her correspondence to Havelock Ellis being read by other eyes alarmed her to the extent that she frequently urged him to destroy what she had written: her importunities at one time became so urgent that he reluctantly destroyed part of his voluminous collection.

> . . . letter-writing [states her husband in the preface to his edition of the letters] was a form of her imperative impulse to express herself to others, and constituted also a mild form of physical exercise . . . Usually such writing was done rapidly, impetuously, carelessly, and almost invariably without any revision or re-reading . . . her letters, even to public persons on important public questions . . . are as careless, undated, often written on odd, unmatched scraps of paper, hard to piece together, as those to her intimate friends. (pp. v–vi)

She wrote, therefore, not a formal literary letter, with a literary effect in mind, but rapidly, to reflect the mood of the moment, to voice her often angry opinions, to give expression to the agonies of her mind, or quieten the restlessness of her disposition, or simply to express her ideas when she could not give herself to the more sustained effort required of serious literary work.

Her letters are spontaneous, robust, alive, penned for the most part in a large scrawling hand. They reveal a mercurial and difficult disposition, beset with all manner of enthusiasm, dislike and change-about. They reveal a woman absorbed by her own illnesses and her morbid fears of her fellow human beings. They reveal a very fallible woman, but someone with powerful emotion, and, though she often deviated from what was best in her, someone with great love. Her husband claims in his selection to have excluded many of her commonplaces. The letters, fortunately, do not seem to have been debilitated by this process: they remain garrulous, repetitious, and characteristic of their author's explosive outbursts.

Olive Schreiner moved from place to place, always restless, hoping to find relief from illness and a place in which she could concentrate on her work, somewhere that she could attain the ideal condition she was always pursuing. Constantly we read that she has settled in a small town in Italy, England or South Africa, is enchanted with it and is working well, to find a few letters later that she has moved: the place oppressed her, brought on her bouts of asthma, which, some writers would have us believe, were as much psychological as physical. The letterheads change from Ratel Hoek and Lelie Kloof in South Africa, to London, to Hastings, to Alassio in Italy, to Mentone, to Matjesfontein back in South Africa, to Johannesburg, Cape Town, Hanover, Beausort West, De Aar, London again, Matjesfontein again, the writer constantly seeking a cure for her illness, always seeking fulfilment, peace and happiness. She finds success, friends, a husband, wonderful scenery, ever turning from one to the other, seeking . . . Trying to write, but never finishing anything to her satisfaction. The letters are a chronicle of her restlessness and the desperate searching of her mind. 'I feel often,' she writes, 'as if too much of the good and joy of life were put into my cup. One must but try to give back what one gets' (p. 11). But shortly afterwards depression claims her: 'Last night I cried for hours, I don't know why. It was like a mad agony come on me' (p. 59). Her life is cramped and frustrated by illness: 'My chest is getting worse . . . now my legs are bad . . . Oh, such hopelessness, such despair . . .' (p. 57). And then, in a flash of insight, she cries out in a letter to Havelock Ellis: 'Oh, it isn't my chest, it isn't my legs, it's I myself, my life. Where shall I go, what shall I do?' (p. 57). A few months later in Portsea Place she writes: 'I'm all ideas, ideas for my book, ideas for my stories; ideas for articles. I am very well' (p. 87). But only two months later she writes to Havelock

Ellis: 'I think I shall go mad . . . I *must* be free, you know, I must be *free*' (p. 90). These changeful moods persist in a correspondence that dates from 1876 to 1920, and occasionally one is forced to meditate: What a waste! Here was a great mind, constantly frustrating itself, burning itself out, by restlessness, lack of sustained concentration, morbid indulgence in illness, hyper-sensitivity to imagined slights.

But Olive Schreiner did work, if somewhat spasmodically. Her writings were not by any manner of means meagre, and some of them show superbly maintained power, something we might not have thought her capable of were we to judge solely by the prevailing tenor of her letters.

Creative writing was no easy matter for her; it drained all her resources, intellectual, emotional and physical. To Havelock Ellis she wrote, obviously impatient with her own limitations (and, possibly, also in justification of what must have seemed a lack of determination and resourcefulness):

> Why don't I get on faster with my work? Why must I write everything with my blood? Other people don't. And I could write in water three novels a year! What is this terrible compulsion over me? (pp. 187–8)

Throughout her letters reference is made to *From Man to Man*. 'The book I am revising now,' she writes early in 1884, 'is the story of a woman, a simple, childlike woman, that goes down, down. I wish, I wish I had more power; I would put it all into this book . . .' (p. 16). In 1886 she writes: 'Will my book ever, ever, ever, be done? Every word of it is truth to me . . .' (p. 98). In 1887 she tells Havelock Ellis: 'Do you know, I'm going to finish my book' (p. 120). In 1889: 'I see my way clear to the end now' (Diary entry, reproduced in S. C. Cronwright-Schreiner's *Life of Olive Schreiner*, p. 182). But in 1907, eighteen years later, the book has not yet been completed and her mood is no longer confident: 'If only the powers that shape existence give me the strength to finish this book, I shall not have that agonised feeling over my life that I have over the last ten years, that I have done nothing of good for any human creature. I am not sure of the book's artistic worth . . .' (pp. 263–4). A month later: 'I am so absorbed and interested in my book I don't like to think of anything else' (p. 264). Three months later: 'Oh, I wish I could get my book done before I die' (p. 268). Olive Schreiner never did finish this book and her husband took it on himself to supply the conclusion.

The Story of an African Farm, Woman and Labour, Thoughts on South Africa, The Buddhist Priest's Wife, and other of her writings are commented on in the letters. She was never self-satisfied; she was often objective and self-critical.

Olive Schreiner was an avid and somewhat promiscuous reader. She is reading a novel; then suddenly she cries out for a biological book – she must have 'facts'; then we find she is reading a book on European history. And so it continues, in characteristic fashion. She has read Hardy's *Far From The Madding Crowd* and writes to Ellis: '. . . it seems to me as though he was only fingering his characters with his hands, not pressing them up against him till he felt their hearts beat' (p. 14). In the same letter she expresses her approval of Ibsen's *The Doll's House*, calling it 'a most wonderful little work' (p. 14). It dealt, of course, with one of Olive Schreiner's pet subjects, the position of woman in society, and her sympathy was readily engaged. Though she was by no means an objective critic, she was always alive to the possibilities of a book. She did not approve of Bernard Shaw, admired Darwin, and considered Gilbert Murray's translations of the Greek tragedies one of the great gifts to her life.

The letters are also interesting in that they manage to reveal much of her relationship with the two great romantic figures in her life, Havelock Ellis and her husband, Cronwright-Schreiner. It is evident that in Cronwright-Schreiner's *Life of Olive Schreiner* and in these letters, which he edited, we have a diluted version of the relationship with Ellis. The fact cannot be disguised, however, that there was a very strong tie between them. Frequently she refers to him as 'My Havelock', or as her 'other self' (e.g. pp. 36 and 152). There are indications that on several occasions he proposed marriage to her, and that she rejected him.

He had read *The Story of an African Farm*, and was struck by the book's lonely genius; its spirit impressed him largely because he had spent years in Australian bush country similar to the world Olive Schreiner described. He wrote to the young author, and on 25th February, 1884, she replied:

> My dear Sir, on my return from a visit to London I found your letter which my publisher had forwarded here. Had I received it sooner I should earlier have written to tell you of the pleasure your expression of sympathy with the little book *An African Farm* gave me. Thank you for having written. (p. 12)

A meeting was arranged, and after she had recovered from her initial disappointment at what she felt was his unprepossessing appearance, their acquaintanceship grew into friendship, and from friendship, whatever her husband would have us believe, into love. On 12th July she is already writing 'You see, dear one . . .' (p. 28). On 9th September: 'It seems to me such a wonderful and sweet thing that you should have come into my life . . .' (p. 41). On 13th October: 'You are the first human being who has been perfect rest to me' (p. 41). On 17th October: 'Don't love me too much' (p. 42). Some months later there are indications that she will not marry him: 'You have taken a place in my life which no marriage or passionate love of mine could ever take from you' (p. 44). Towards the end of the year she says 'I belong to you', but talks now of their *friendship*, and tells him that 'Now I know I cannot fall in love' (p. 50). The following year she assures him 'If you are made unhappy by the thought of my marrying, that needn't be, because I shall never marry anyone' (p. 80). In 1886 she re-emphasizes her attitude in rejecting a proposal of marriage from Dr Brian Donkin: 'I can't marry, Henry, I can't . . . I *must* be free, you know, I must be *free*' (p. 90). Her tie with Havelock Ellis continued throughout their lives, their correspondence including many hundreds of letters, and even in 1914 we find her writing to him: 'I love you, dear' (p. 344).

Almost one of the first intimations we receive in her correspondence of the existence of Cronwright-Schreiner is when on 16th February, 1894, she writes to Havelock Ellis: 'My old Havelock, I'm going to be married on Saturday morning, the 24th' (p. 213). On 7th March she has been married thirteen days and she writes to Miss Louie Ellis: 'I hope I shall have a little baby, Louie, but if I don't I shall be satisfied too' (p. 214). She speaks of her love for Cronwright, how infinitely beautiful life is, and how strong she feels. 'Marriage, perfect marriage of mind and body, is such a lovely and holy thing . . .' (p. 217). From a letter to Mrs J. H. Philpot on 8th August we gather that she is pregnant. All the indications are that she will settle down – she has a devoted husband, a home, and is to have a child. But in April the darkness descends again on Olive Schreiner's life – the baby she has waited for so long (she was almost forty) dies the day after its birth. For months afterwards she cannot bear to think of it, but is constantly reminded of what she has lost. She visits Mrs Solly in Kimberley and writes to Cronwright about it:

> There were some lovely likenesses of a baby . . . It was so like our baby. When Mrs Solly came into the room I introduced myself, and said a few words and said what a pretty baby it was in the likeness, and then I burst out crying and had to go away . . . (p. 222)

Her restlessness begins in earnest again: she cannot live at Cronwright's farm Krantz Plaats – it affects her asthma. De Aar and Beaufort West prove equally unsuitable, and the rest of her life is a series of separations from and coming together with Cronwright. In the last year of her life, they meet in London after a separation of several years, only for Olive to return almost immediately to South Africa. But to the very end her protestations of love for her husband have not diminished. On 29th February, 1920, she writes to him: 'You know I can't really realise you are coming. I think I'll die with joy . . .' (p. 367). Yet within weeks they part and Cronwright never sees his wife again. She dies, alone, in a Cape Town boarding-house. Yet, during her life and after it, by his sacrifices to her unattainable comfort and by his painstaking editing of her work, Cronwright shows himself to be a dedicated husband.

She had many missions in life – one was for women, another for peace, another for truth – and they all are given expression in her letters. Though in a sense Olive Schreiner was a citizen of the world (and this long before the concept became popular), she was by no means a fence-sitter. In fact she made herself extremely unpopular by refusing to commit herself to any causes except those that thoroughly compelled her faith – and some of these to people governed by stereotyped emotions no doubt seemed wayward and perverse. 'Oh, this is a wicked wicked war,' she wrote in 1899 of the South African Boer War. 'When I see our bonny English boys falling . . . and our own brave South African lads dying while the [word not printed by her husband] who worked up the thing go to their garden parties and lounge about with their cigars and champagne, a bitterness rises in my heart that I never thought could' (pp. 228–9). The banners of patriotism could to her be the tokens of wanton and hypocritical bloodshed. In 1914 she was in England, speaking out fearlessly against the Great War, and being ostracised for her stand. 'Why has one always to stand alone?' she wrote to Havelock Ellis. 'Why can one never go with the tide of the mob?' (p. 338).

In spite of Olive Schreiner's restlessness and her preoccupation with her recurring illnesses – remarks such as 'the fight for breath is quite habitual now' proliferate in her letters – we feel that the central struggle of her life towards truth is never really blurred by the distractions that beset her. Indeed she herself did not feel that her life had been without direction. 'Everyone will say again I am wandering without a motive,' she writes. 'I have never moved without a motive . . .' (p. 158). Constantly her fight has been against 'that side of human nature which wants not truth, but ease' (p. 306), and her own life was not easy on that account. Constantly she is opposing herself to the blind acceptance of conventional religion, because for so many people it is not the way of hard truth, but an easy escape from reality. '. . . truth is before all things' (p. 18) she wrote early in her life (1884), and this credo still held good for her in 1920.

'What a man may do, each soul, is to exert a tiny influence in the direction good and beautiful to him . . .' (p. 226). There was much about her imperfect struggles that was inspiring, and even reassuring. '. . . I can sympathise,' she writes, 'with all the lives, with all the endeavours, with all the accomplished work, even with all the work attempted and not accomplished, of other men' (p. 227). It is more than possible that she secretly hoped that those following after her would feel much the same about her life. She did not, however, cherish any illusions about her failure to realise her possibilities, and despite her declamations against her illness and the inconsiderateness of other people, she knew that no one was to blame but herself. 'Somehow all my life seems a mistake to me now, and no one else all through to blame but I' (p. 116). She pleads excuses for her failures, asks forgiveness, but she has failed because she is herself: '. . . *character is persistent*' (p. 225), she writes, and even earlier, '. . . I haven't power . . . to be otherwise than as I am' (p. 115). But her faith in the quality of effort remains undimmed. She writes to her husband of her work:

> . . . there is not one word that stands there, which, if it had been in my power to better it, would not have been bettered. If I feel I have not expressed the exact truth that is in me in any line or sentence or book, it shall be destroyed . . . (p. 225)

She has failed, she has succeeded, she has known truth – yet she cannot really understand herself; her conflicts, struggles and failures are to her inexplicable, part of a terrible but at the same time wonderful mystery. 'I don't understand myself now,' she writes to Havelock Ellis in 1885, 'and how should you? In years to come I will see what was the meaning of all this' (p. 66). But from her letters it is quite clear that she never did.

THE HAVELOCK ELLIS-OLIVE SCHREINER
MANUSCRIPT COLLECTION
(Humanities Research Center, University of Texas, Austin)

Though the edition of Olive Schreiner's letters published by her husband has undoubted value (as the first of these notes has tried to indicate) it also has serious gaps, is excessively edited, and can be misleading to those seeking the truth about the life of this famous writer. The published selection must be supplemented by an examination of unpublished documents, or of documents incompletely or imperfectly reproduced by Cronwright-Schreiner.

There are some sources in South Africa – such as those at the University of Cape Town[1] or at the small municipal library of Cradock in the Eastern Province – that no doubt require further exploration, but the purpose of this note is to point to an amazing collection outside South Africa, where much that is highly relevant to Olive Schreiner's story awaits the investigator. The Havelock Ellis-Olive Schreiner collection of the Humanities Research Center of the University of Texas, Austin, consists of nearly four hundred letters, most of which have never been reproduced in their complete or correct form. What follows is a suggestion of their potentiality, and is based on an examination of only those few letters consulted by the writer during a brief visit to Texas in 1966.

An examination of the following three extracts suggests something of the disadvantage under which biographers have hitherto laboured:

1. From *The Letters of Olive Schreiner*, edited by Cronwright-Schreiner:

   If I am to live I must be free, and under existing circumstances I feel more and more that no kind of sex relationship can be good and pure but marriage. – is so tender and sweet and reverent to me. My heart aches when I think I can never marry him. (p. 90)

2. In the latest and, by his own assertion, the most definitive of the biographies (*Olive Schreiner: Portrait of a South African Woman*), Johannes Meintjes manages to identify the anony-

---

1. The most important of the several collections in the Jagger Library of the University of Cape Town is probably that comprising over four hundred letters from Olive Schreiner to her brother W. P. Schreiner, who – as Chapter I records – played a prominent part in Cape history, and was at one time Prime Minister of the Cape Colony.

mous '–' of Cronwright-Schreiner's collection, but with the exception of one typographical difference reproduces the passage as it is printed:

If I am to live I must be free, and under existing circumstances I feel more and more that no kind of sex relationship can be good and pure but marriage. X is so tender and sweet and reverent to me. My heart aches when I think I can never marry him. (p. 89)

3. The manuscript in the Humanities Research Center reads as follows:

If I am to live I must be free, and under existing circumstances I feel *more* and *more* that no kind of sex relationship can be good and pure but marriage. Dr Donkin is so tender and sweet to me [,] will not even touch my lips reverently unless he is quite sure I wish it, and my heart aches for him when I think I can never marry him.

The differences may, initially, seem unimportant, but when considered in terms of an extensive collection, they suggest omissions and deviations that could be considerable. In the context of Olive Schreiner's attitude to marriage, sex and feminism, even the brief reference to Donkin's reticence becomes illuminating. And in the unemphatic sounding of the 'more and more' of the published volumes we have lost something of the garrulous passion with which she urged on her arguments.

The whole story of Havelock Ellis and Olive Schreiner will no doubt never be known, but the hundreds of letters exchanged between them that are now in the Humanities Research Center offer more of the truth than Cronwright-Schreiner's *Life* or the edited correspondence, and more than Havelock Ellis's autobiography.

The letters examined by the present writer throw sharp light on Olive Schreiner's life in England in the eighteen-eighties, and on her association with several notable men of the day. Not only is her relationship with Havelock Ellis loquaciously explored, but also her dealings with Edward Carpenter and Dr Brian Donkin (who proposed marriage to her several times). There are some emphatic, if not fully explicit, statements about her attitude to Professor Karl Pearson, for whom she confesses a love which, she then proceeds to insist, is *not* physical.

Although the platonic side of love is much emphasised, her interesting attitudes – and those of Havelock Ellis – to sexual love, enjoy an openness of discussion, if not singular, at least uncommon at the time in which they wrote. Despite her passionate temperament sexual relationships were for her far more complicated than mere acts of submission; the conflicts that beset her constitute one of the most fascinating aspects of the spontaneous discourses in which she felt compelled to indulge.

The complexity and persistence of Havelock Ellis's love (and there is no reason to suppose it ungenuine) emerge through the accumulation of the correspondence. Olive Schreiner had quite clearly decided that there could be no talk of marriage between them – in fact, rather insensitively, she discussed her other love (though not necessarily sexual) relationships with him, and she sometimes suggested his marrying someone else. On at least one occasion he was stung to a retort:

> It is mere unthinking cruelty for you to talk about my being happy and marrying . . .

He goes on to add:

> Coming home last night I thought that I should be able to be happy if *you* were married . . .

Later, having discussed their personal infelicity in rather frank terms, he continues:

> Tear this up at once. I shan't want to see you so much after writing this.

He seems here to have expressed not a wish to discontinue their association, but a satisfaction at having been able to *talk* to her in the form of a letter (and many of their notes do suggest conversation rather than correspondence), for only a few lines later he concludes as follows:

> Do you want me to bring you anything on Friday? [I] *do* trust and understand you, darling.

This undated letter is characteristic of the strange vacillations of their relationship, though Ellis's protestations of love are un-remitting. Despite the fact that his emotional statements are laboriously involved, and often repetitious, we never cease being moved to sympathy by cries such as the following:

> Ever since I left you I have had a dull aching sensation it [in] my heart. I don't know what it is . . . Oh Olive, Olive, Olive. (Letter dated 29.8.84)

Or:

> My heart wants you. It feels dead when it isn't near you. (Letter dated 30.8.84)

Olive Schreiner would frequently respond with a feeling equal to his:

> Harry come, and I'll make that heart glad, that sweet tender heart that longs so for love. Ach Harry. Don't feel sad my sweetheart there so far away from me.

This could be the manner of a mother comforting her child, and yet – uncannily – they are both like infants caught in the vastness of an emotional storm they only partially comprehend: this impression is conveyed, amongst other things, by involuntary interjections such as 'Ach Harry' or 'Oh Olive, Olive, Olive'. They continually examined the sexuality, or the lack of it, in their relationship, but what becomes clear (to the present writer, at least) was that this was not a literary pose, or one of those sentimental excursions in which late Victorianism sometimes liked to indulge: it was the struggle of two honest people surveying not only the tangle of a curious emotional involvement, but the workings of an ill-understood universe and the perpetual ambivalences of animality and its absence.

Although one treads with caution when one intrudes into the private lives of human beings – even those long since dead – the Havelock Ellis-Olive Schreiner correspondence invites detailed and sympathetic examination: it tells the remarkable story of two remarkable human beings.

A. THE WORKS OF OLIVE SCHREINER

1. NOVELS

The Story of an African Farm. London, Chapman and Hall, 1883. Published under the name of Ralph Iron. A dramatisation, by Merton Hodge, of *The Story of an African Farm* appeared in 1939 (London, Heinemann).

Undine. New York, and London, Harper, 1929. Published post-humously.

Trooper Peter Halket of Mashonaland. London, Unwin, 1897.

From Man to Man; or, Perhaps Only. London, Unwin, 1926. Published posthumously.

2. SHORT STORIES

Dream and Real Life. London, Unwin, 1893. (Pseudonym Library). Published under the name of Ralph Iron.

    Contents: Dream Life and Real Life – A Little African Story; The Woman's Rose; The Policy in Favour of Protection.

Stories, Dreams and Allegories. London, Unwin, 1923. Published posthumously.

    Contents: Stories: Eighteen-Ninety-Nine; The Buddhist Priest's Wife; On the Banks of a Full River; The Wax Doll and the Stepmother; The Adventures of Master Towser. *Dreams and Allegories:* A Soul's Journey; God's Gifts to Man; They Heard; Life's Gifts; The Flower and the Spirit; The River of Life; The Brown Flower; The Two Paths; A Dream of Prayer; Workers; The Cry of South Africa; Seeds A-growing; The Great Heart of England; Who Knocks at the Door?; The Winged Butterfly. *The 1924 edition also includes:* The Dawn of Civilisation.

Dreams. London, Unwin, 1890.
> *Contents:* The Lost Joy; The Hunter (From: *The Story of an African Farm*); The Gardens of Pleasure; In a Far-Off World; Three Dreams in a Desert; A Dream of Wild Bees (Written as a letter to a friend); In a Ruined Chapel; Life's Gifts; The Artist's Secret; I Thought I Stood; The Sunlight Lay Across my Bed.

Stories, Dreams and Allegories
> See under SHORT STORIES.

4. POLITICS

Thoughts on South Africa. London, Unwin, 1923. Published post-humously.
> *Contents:* South Africa, its Natural Features, etc; The Boer; The Problem of Slavery; The Wanderings of the Boer; The Boer Woman and the Modern Woman's Question; The Boer and his Republics; The Psychology of the Boer; The Englishman.
> *Appendices:* The South African Nation; The Value of Human Varieties; The Domestic Life of the Boer; Our Waste Land in Mashonaland.

An English South African's View of the Situation; Words in Season. London, Hodder and Stoughton, 1899.

Closer Union; a Letter on the South African Union and the Principles of Government. London, Fifield, 1909. A reprint in pamphlet form of her letter to *The Transvaal Leader* (22nd December, 1908, p. 6).

The Political Situation. London, Unwin, 1896. Written jointly with S. C. Cronwright-Schreiner.

A Letter on the Jew. Cape Town, Liberman, 1906.

Woman and Labour. London, and Leipzig, Unwin, 1911.

The Letters of Olive Schreiner, 1876–1920; edited by S. C. Cronwright-Schreiner. London, Unwin, 1924. Published posthumously.

Appendices: Speech on the Boer War, Cape Town, July 1900; Letter on Boer War, Paarl women's meeting, 1900; Speech on Boer War, Somerset East women's meeting, 1900; Letter read at Johannesburg shop assistants' demonstration, 1905 (?); Letter on 'The Taal', reprinted from *Cape Times*, 10th May, 1905; 'Letter on the Jew' (extracts from); Letter on women's suffrage read at public meeting, Cape Town, May 1908; 'Conscientious objectors', reprinted from *Labour Leader*, London, 16th March, 1916; Letter to peace meeting, London, 1916; Letter to women's meeting in commemoration of John Stuart Mill, London, 1918.

B. WORKS ON OLIVE SCHREINER

1. ANTHOLOGIES

NUTTALL, Neville *editor*

    The Silver Plume; a Selection From the Writings of Olive Schreiner. Johannesburg, Afrikaanse Pers Beperk, 1957.

    Extracts from: Dream Life and Real Life; Dreams; Stories, Dreams and Allegories; Woman and Labour; Thoughts on South Africa; From Man to Man; The Story of an African Farm.

KRIGE, Uys *editor*

    Olive Schreiner: a Selection. Cape Town, Oxford University Press, 1968.

Extracts from: The Story of an African Farm; Stories, Dreams and Allegories; Trooper Peter Halket of Mashonaland; Woman and Labour; From Man to Man, or Perhaps Only ...; Thoughts on South Africa; A Letter on the Jew; Closer Union; Letters.

THURMAN, Howard *editor*
A Track to the Water's Edge: the Olive Schreiner Reader. New York, Harper and Row, 1973.

2. BIBLIOGRAPHIES

VERSTER, E. *compiler*
Olive Emilie Albertina Schreiner (1855–1920): *Bibliography.* Cape Town, University of Cape Town, 1946.

DAVIS, Roslyn *compiler*
Olive Schreiner, 1920–1971: a Bibliography. Johannesburg, University of the Witwatersrand, 1972.

3. BIOGRAPHY AND CRITICISM

CRONWRIGHT-SCHREINER, S. C.
The Life of Olive Schreiner. London, Unwin, 1924.

BUCHANAN-GOULD, Vera
Not Without Honour: the Life and Writings of Olive Schreiner London, Hutchinson, 1948.

FRIEDMANN, Marion V.
Olive Schreiner: a Study in Latent Meanings. Johannesburg, Witwatersrand University Press, 1954.

HOBMAN, D. L.
Olive Schreiner: Her Friends and Times. London, Watts and Co., 1955.

GREGG, Lyndall (Dot Schreiner)
Memories of Olive Schreiner. London, W. and R. Chambers, 1957.

MEINTJES, Johannes

Olive Schreiner: Portrait of a South African Woman. Johannesburg, Hugh Keartland, 1965.

FRIEDLANDER, Zelda *editor*

Until the Heart Changes: a Garland for Olive Schreiner. Cape Town, Tafelberg-uitgewers, 1967.

Sections on: The Woman; The Family; The Reformer; The Writer.

OLIVE SCHREINER: A SELECTION
edited by Uys Krige

This volume, which must in many ways be regarded as the most acceptable (if by no means the definitive) selection from Olive Schreiner's work, could have enjoyed greater care in its editing. That Bonaparte Blenkins should be referred to five times on page 8 as 'Napoleon Blenkins' is perhaps a small fault, but inexcusable when one considers the authority this book will command (if only by virtue of its eminent publisher). The available evidence, both external and textual, points to *Undine* as an earlier work than *The Story of an African Farm*, and to claim for it the status of a later, poor novel is to do its author a great injustice (a greater injustice when one realises that Olive Schreiner entreated Havelock Ellis to destroy the manuscript, and that her husband – perhaps unknowingly – did precisely the opposite in publishing it).[1] The short story Uys Krige calls 'Two Women' (not included in the collection because of its length) can only be that published by her husband as 'Eighteen-Ninety-Nine'. Krige does not produce his authority for this change of title. (Incidentally, I agree that this is by far Olive Schreiner's best short story.)

I find Krige's account of her fiction and its weaknesses a little too easy:

> Perhaps [he writes] the main fault of *The Story of an African Farm* flows from the fact that Olive Schreiner is not basically a novelist but a poet, highly individual and subjective with all the passionately intense inner life characteristic of the poet's unique personality. (p. 1)

How comfortable it would be to account for those long interludes and interruptions in *An African Farm* by calling them the discursions of a lyrical poet. Krige's label does of course in part

---

1. See the section on *Undine* (Chapter II).

account for a characteristically compelling and also, perversely, an irritating aspect of the book's achievement, but I believe that *An African Farm* can quite easily stand up to examination – even if not consistently favourable – as a novel, and that in passages such as that in which Waldo sits in the 'red sand' carving a piece of wood and attracts from a stranger a tale about the white bird of truth, we have more than merely poetic vigour. They can be fitted without undue effort (and with a certain reward) into the structure and meaning of the novel. Krige finds the two Strangers weakening, even meaningless to the book. Surely they are intentional to the fable the novelist was contriving – Olive Schreiner herself accounts for their presence, in her Preface to the second edition, when she refers to 'a strange coming and going of feet'.[2]

Krige's comments are, however, attractively, zestfully forthright, for example when he cannot understand why (in that famous, oft-quoted conclusion) Waldo 'a strong, healthy young man . . . should, in the last page of the book, lie down in the sun and just die . . .' (p. 4). I feel he has missed a point, but what it is I cannot remember – and perhaps his objection is, after all, a valid one.

Although I continue to resist the poetic clamp in which he wishes to place the book, his poetry thesis gives impetus to some of his best remarks about *An African Farm*. We feel his own South African blood coursing wildly in response to Olive Schreiner's superb evocation:

> . . . the book should be seen rather as a poem than as a novel; a poem written by a young woman hardly out of her teens in which – often deeply disturbed by the sudden violences, griefs and exaltations of her emotional, still-adolescent nature, tortured by her agonising insight into the modern woman's needs in a hostile male world, racked by her 'thirst for the absolute', her profound doubts in the God of her fathers, and yearning for the full life waiting for her beyond the wide circle of those far, blue koppies – she speaks of her

2. See p. 19.

sorrows and ecstasies in so pure and passionate a voice that criticism is silenced.

And nowhere is her poet's gift more apparent than in her evocative power. How this African farm lives! How clearly one sees it, even when it is not directly described but its presence or atmosphere only suggested: shimmering, almost afloat in the haze of early summer; distorted into a phantas-magoria of shape and contour, sky, land and water in the drought's mocking mirage; etched in the sharp white light of winter; fresh and with a fragrance of its own in the desert dawn; parched and bleak in the hot glare of noon; glowing in the immense golden and crimson sunset; or touched at night to a still, mysterious beauty by the moon. (pp. 4–5)

Because Krige is so impressed by the author's powers of evocation, I cannot understand his omission of Olive Schreiner's pictures of the farm by night and by day, unless he felt that they were unsubtle as descriptions, or that they had been too often quoted and anthologised.

His main contention – and it is a highly valid one, though subject to important qualification – is that Olive Schreiner's decisive gift lay with non-fiction: her hard, panoramic thinking was epitomised in clear, forceful prose. Of *Woman and Labour* he says:

. . . Olive Schreiner's supple, swift prose has here such a sustained power, such a Karoo-like cleanness and clarity [what an attractive Krige-like analogy this is!] that much of it is as readable today as it must have been on its first appearance.

Quotation by no means does justice to its peculiar quality. Coming with acute observation upon acute observation, piling telling argument upon telling argument, giving time and again striking proof of the wide range of her mind . . . (p. 8)

If this is true of *Woman and Labour* how much more so it is of Olive Schreiner's undoubted masterpiece *Thoughts on South Africa*. Krige's analysis of this book is particularly admirable. In the present survey I have pointed to her gift of prophecy, which had its basis in the exacting thinking of which, despite her vagaries, she was capable.[3] It is her role of prophet that has particular, and deserved, emphasis in Krige's examination of *Thoughts on South Africa*. He indicates her impressive political output in his telling references to writings such as *Closer Union* (written in 1908) and 'Conscientious Objectors' (1916).[4] In fact Krige will have it – and I tend to agree with him – that her reputation should be based not on *An African Farm*, but on her political output:

> Who [he argues] of all our South African writers – or any writer on South Africa and South African conditions for that matter – has expressed these truths more passionately and yet at the same time more cogently and logically? (p. 24)

He does not have a very high opinion of the dreams, and this opinion is in part reinforced by the selection he has made (though I do not for a moment suggest that he subjected the anthology to his thesis). He has omitted some allegories that have considerable force of prophecy: I am thinking particularly here of 'The Sunlight Lay Across My Bed' and 'Who Knocks at the Door?'.

The selections from *An African Farm*, on the other hand, bear out many of the favourable claims he makes for them. For example 'The Sacrifice' is a particularly fine piece of writing, though I think abbreviated passages such as 'Waldo's Confession' are too brief to give the proper impact – and it is here more a novelist's impact than a poetic one. There are some omissions I am a little sad about: for example, the two descriptions of the farm (referred to above), Waldo's meeting with his stranger, Waldo and Lyndall in discussion under the stars at the Boer wedding (both the immediate and the distant are here splendidly linked, as they are in the discussion that takes place), Waldo's return after his father's death (one of the most macabre portraits of Bonaparte Blenkins, incidentally), and his return to Em near the end of the novel.[5] But the passages Krige has selected demonstrate anew

3. See pp. 61–2.

4. See the Bibliography (*The Letters of Olive Schreiner*).

5. See pp. 19–20, and 22–7.

that the writer had a power critics tend to underrate. This gift is apparent even in so small a touch as the following (from 'Waldo's Machine'). Waldo has proudly been describing his invention to Bonaparte Blenkins, who appears to think highly of it. Then Bonaparte, suggesting a small improvement,

. . . put his foot on the machine and crushed it into the sand.

The boy looked up into his face. (p. 43)

This last short sentence has, in its context and in the context of the entire novel, an understatement and a poignancy that are deeply moving. (Later in the passage where Olive Schreiner seeks to adumbrate the 'life-situation' in the image of the dog killing the beetle (p. 44) her writing becomes self-conscious and gauche – she was not a skilful contriver of conscious imagery. The imagery that came from her imaginative involvement would seldom fail.)

Most of the selections are very thoughtful, particularly those from the political writings. The following extract from a letter (2.11.1888) to Havelock Ellis could serve as an effective text to the main theme both of Krige's Introduction and his Selection:

It's so easy for a mind like mine to produce long logical arguments, or strings of assertions, but when I have done it I feel such a 'walg' against it: that is only the material; it has to be combined and made alive. (p. 196)

Olive Schreiner only spasmodically brought her arguments to life and gave them coherence in her creative work (that is, her fiction); she was amazingly sustained in giving life and coherence to her arguments in her expository writing (writing which serves to demonstrate a truly creative attitude, and also how misleading these labels can be – a third-rate novelist, for example, rarely deserves the appellation of 'creative'. Incidentally – while I am in a parenthesis – Krige uses the word 'walg' in his Introduction to show how Olive Schreiner sometimes did her thinking in Afrikaans (p. 21). I believe she was highly conscious of Afrikaans vocabulary, and gave it great currency in English, but I do not for a moment believe she was able to think in Afrikaans, even at an elementary level. She had tremendous sympathy for, and imaginative insight into, Afrikaner attitudes, and these were the things that would carry her far into the realm of proper interpretation.)

Krige in his examination of *From Man to Man* presents the tragedy of her largely unrealised gift; a tragedy that was manifest in much of her writing (particularly in her letters) and in the quarrels and the restless, unsated wanderings of which so much of her life seemed to consist. His picture of her on her solitary walks in the war-torn London of 1914–18 is a very touching one. And yet (at a time when, as I have suggested, there is currency for the contention that she is overrated) Krige manages to bring out her fierce independence as a South African and as a genuine world-citizen. The heroic, generous truth she sought would, in less stereotyped and vituperative times than our own, have been sufficient to establish nationality – and internationality.

Uys Krige's main purpose in undertaking this selection is of course to pay accurate tribute to Olive Schreiner. The following two extracts from the Introduction show something of the quality of his endeavour:

Besides her gifts of foresight Olive Schreiner was also blessed – the weak or timorous, or certain dabblers in psychology who must, it seems, always diminish the superior man or woman among us by ascribing to his or her best actions a mean or even ignoble motive, might well say 'cursed' – with the qualities of the hero: not the hero of the single heroic act who is often moved by an impulse of a purely ephemeral nature or sustained by what he feels strongly to be the wholehearted approval of his fellows; but the hero of a rarer kind, the hero who, though the heroic temper be of his very essence, has to achieve that heroism for himself repeatedly in crisis after crisis; the hero who, when confronted as Olive Schreiner so often was with a great moral crisis or a tragic conflict in the life of his people, does not reckon the gain or loss but, despite the fiercest opposition and his own intense spiritual suffering because of the split in his personal relationships caused by such a crisis or conflict, continues to speak and act unequivocally for truth or righteousness as he sees it. (p. 24)

If it is true, as Olive Schreiner said herself many years before, that 'it is easier for a man to die than to stand alone', then she had indeed died many times in the course of her lonely, wandering and so often bitterly frustrated, life – but always to live again, fearlessly, in the proud independence of her indomitable spirit, in her scorn of the false, the mean and the ignoble, in her ceaseless battle for what she thought good and just; and in her shining faith in humanity and man's infinite possibilities. (p. 30)

THE LIFE OF OLIVE SCHREINER
by S. C. Cronwright-Schreiner

Cronwright-Schreiner should not be held entirely to blame for the failure of his *Life of Olive Schreiner*: the book fails because it cannot capture the genius, and becomes a chronicle of the life of an eccentric; it portrays the neurotic but fails to convey to us the torrential personality of the artist. Cronwright was curiously unfitted for his task. On the one hand he was mesmerised by the brilliant mind of the genius who accepted him; on the other he was disgruntled, and tired of the woman who disappointed him. Add to this, that he was, despite his fine qualities, a very ordinary man who was not able really to understand the character of her gifts and concomitant disposition. Time and again the book vacillates between eulogy and a resentful petulance. 'She did not seem to remember that I had taken the grave step of giving up my livelihood at her special request in order that she might finish and publish *The Buddhist Priest's Wife* and *From Man to Man*' (p. 287), he writes of the period after their marriage. Resentment and disappointment seem to have set in when Olive Schreiner failed to produce the steady stream of masterpieces he had expected of her. The book is filled with these strange recriminations against his wife and justifications of himself.

> I have always felt that in Olive I had a sacred trust and that it would be almost criminal if any act of mine should prevent her writing. I had to give her the chance, it seemed to me, at almost any cost to myself. I did not know her so well then as I did later, her impracticability, her inability really to work . . . (p. 269)

Page after page smoulders with an obtuse resentment – then he seems to remember his duty to the genius he has made his life's burden, and he takes flight on the wings of eulogy: '. . . for the last time I had looked on the woman, who, of all human creatures, had my admiration, my love, and my deep reverence; for the last time I had heard that wonderful voice; for the last time gazed on those unearthly luminous eyes' (p. 377). Certainly his must have been a trying and disappointing role. 'If there were *any* conditions,' he writes exasperatedly, 'under which she could work steadily for some time I do not know them' (p. 303).

The overall effect of this book is that of a tired labour of love, 'the task I have set myself' (p. 366), as he describes it. It gives the effect of being laboriously methodical: at great length he deals with her ancestry and brothers and sisters; he carefully charters the walks she took on the Ganna Hoek farms; but fails, pitifully at times, to breathe life into what he has to tell us. Despite its care, his chronology is not always faultless either; for example, Olive Schreiner is recorded as having her twenty-first birthday in two successive years (pp. 103 and 118). Much of the book is painfully slow going, and in its grim seriousness, unconsciously funny: 'She had a magnificent chest . . .' (p. 90).

Cronwright gives the impression that he was buried under the mass of detail with which the material at his disposal provided him, and that he had not the equipment of a great or even a competent writer to deal with it: '. . . our fate was cast for the next five years at Hanover . . .' he writes. 'I will summarise our time there under several heads' (p. 332). This type of writing gives a dated and stilted effect to the book.

The statement made earlier that he deals with her eccentricities rather than her genius, that from his pages a neurotic woman emerges who was hardly likely to influence her contemporaries in any way, needs enlargement. '. . . she was a woman of genius, so strange and incredible in her personality . . . that I doubted whether it [her life] could be conveyed in writing' (p. vii), he states in his preface. He explains her 'strange' and 'incredible' behaviour as signs of mental brilliance, in tones almost of awe, while all they reveal is a rather trying neurotic. As a child, if unjustly treated 'she used to get under the bed and bang her head against the wall until she was almost senseless' (p. 68). As a woman at 'a knock at the door . . . she would hide under the table . . .'

(p. 68). 'On receipt of a telegram . . . the moment she had read it, she would put it with a quick motion into her mouth and chew it rapidly . . .' (p. 166). She used to walk through the house at the dead of night slamming doors, even though her husband was trying to sleep after a hard day's work.

> She took violent dislikes to some people. Mrs . . . called to see her in my house at Burghersdorp and almost at once they began to quarrel, and were quite rude to each other; Olive hated her; the second time she called they sparred at each other, and Olive sprang up and banged the door in her face. (p. 79)

And so the narrative continues, often faintly interesting, sometimes grimly amusing, but hardly a balanced portrait of a woman who had such profound impact on her contemporaries.

That she did have such an impact there can be little reason to doubt, especially after having read the testimonies of people who knew her. Rhodes admired her deeply; she and Paul Kruger became friends; for some time Havelock Ellis was devoted to her. Arthur Symons speaks of the great women of the world and feels 'that Olive Schreiner is the greatest of them all. The George Sands, George Eliots pale before her incredible ardency' (p. 185). Women were inspired by her. '. . . by the flashlight of Olive's genius,' writes Mrs John Brown, '. . . one saw a step in the road that leads one upward' (p. 184). 'Her personality and her influence were indeed magnetic' (p. 364) – from a newspaper account of a dinner in London at which she spoke. But, and this is the pity, although these high estimates of Olive Schreiner are quoted frequently, and often at length, her husband fails to bring *this* woman to life.

Part of the effect she had on people can be attributed to the fact that she was a vivid, forceful conversationalist. According to her friend, Mrs Hemming, 'she talked brilliantly, got very excited at times, and to me was most fascinating' (p. 79). She was a person of 'great presence', with 'powerful gestures . . . blaze of eye and explosive energy . . .' (p. 22). '. . . she became on subjects that interested her,' wrote Havelock Ellis, 'an eloquent talker, and, finally, dogmatic and intolerant of contradiction . . .' (p. 161).

Some measure of honour must be bestowed on Cronwright, however, for giving her views ample (and, for the most part, intelligently edited) expression. There are massive quotations from her journal, her letters, and other of her writings. An interesting feature of these quotations is that while in her formal writing she was a careful and exacting thinker, 'testing the validity of every idea before she made it her own',[1] her letters usually produce the impression of an unstable, though strong, personality. Her utterances in her letters are unsystematic, contradictory and with no respect for facts or chronology; her husband corrects her on numerous occasions in the form of asides, although, as we have seen, he himself is not so careful a chronologist as he would have us think. Occasionally in snatches of her letters and journals the spirit of Olive Schreiner's yearning reaches us. 'Horrible desire for immortality last night,' she writes in 1880; 'hope I shall die suddenly. Anything else is easily given up for truth – except immortality' (p. 141). Although she quarrelled with those around her: 'I mean to try and love every person and every thing and to look for the good' (p. 139).

The impression of her too-fallible humanity is reinforced by Cronwright's incessant contradiction of her statements about herself; it is made clear in this book that he learnt by bitter experience that she was not accurate in her statements, except in those she revised and gave to the world in published form (although he does also question (p. 354) the validity of her published account of a predecessor to *Woman and Labour*).

This is not a good biography because Cronwright was not, could not be, completely accurate and impartial in his portrait of his wife; he was limited by his very nearness to her. Havelock Ellis's role is sketchily treated, and the suggestion that they were in love at any time, carefully blinked at. He is brought in only

---

1. Partridge, A. C. *editor. Readings in South African English Prose*. Pretoria, J. L. van Schaik, 1948 (second, revised edition). Introduction, by the editor, p. 15.

for a few pages, where he writes a carefully worded little tribute. In fact this whole record of Olive Schreiner's relations with Havelock Ellis and Cronwright-Schreiner lacks balance: her life with Cronwright is carefully chronicled and made much of, while her relation to Havelock Ellis is studiously underplayed. Cronwright-Schreiner was not in a position to tell the whole truth.

The difficulty of writing an objective biography is well-expressed in Olive Schreiner's own words. 'Truth,' she wrote to an intemperate journalist who had attempted some personal record of her work and life, 'is much too large a thing in this great mysterious universe for any individual to believe he holds it all in his single hand' (p. 299).

NOT WITHOUT HONOUR: THE LIFE AND WRITINGS OF OLIVE SCHREINER
by Vera Buchanan-Gould

In this biography Vera Buchanan-Gould set out to do too much. She set out to do Olive Schreiner more than justice, to prove once and for all that she was a greater woman than she really was. But the subject rebels against the treatment, contradicts the eulogies.

The approach in this biography tends to leave one feeling apathetic, and this is a pity because the author's object was the reverse. The eulogies are so frequent and occasionally so exasperatingly uncritical that they become, frankly, tiresome. Olive Schreiner's husband is guilty of the same excesses, but he has a greater claim to exoneration, one feels, because he was less fortunately placed, both in space and time, than Vera Buchanan-Gould to construct a balanced portrait of this erratic genius-woman.

In some ways Vera Buchanan-Gould was fighting a mythical battle. It was her passionate conviction that Olive Schreiner's stocks are very low – on the contrary, I find them very high, especially among those people who do not know her work, who regard her as a mysterious but glittering comet, streaking across the late nineteenth century with her *Story of an African Farm*, a gigantic masterpiece which, almost invariably, they have not troubled to read. I have tried to indicate that Olive Schreiner had a considerable mind, at her best a beautiful and forceful prose style, and a compelling and strong personality, but continually to place her in the misty upper regions is to do her a grave injustice.

Statements such as the following need very definite substantiation if they are not to be dismissed as merely excessive: '. . . Olive Schreiner raised this theme [sexual injustice to woman] from the swamps of sentimentality to the stormy, abiding peaks of tragedy' (p. 73). That 'Lyndall is, possibly, the first heroine of fiction who can really be compared to Shakespeare's tragic heroes' (p. 79), is so wildly extravagant a claim that one is inclined to question all Vera Buchanan-Gould's judgements. However valuable 'The Sunlight Lay across my Bed' is, I feel that an assertion that 'perhaps no greater condemnation of the utter unconcern of the rich for the sufferings of the poor has ever been penned' (p. 110) simply does not belong in literary criticism. Her comparison of Olive Schreiner with Christ, Socrates and Wagner also does her mission little good. (And this is a sparse selection; similar judgements abound in the book.)

One regrets that her statements tend to become so uncritical, because, on the whole, in her discussion of Olive Schreiner's writings she makes the woman and her work appear significant; she successfully brings out the main themes in the books, the impulses and objects behind them, and, also, some very good reason for their value. Of *Woman and Labour* she makes the following statement, which is a very articulate estimate of Olive Schreiner's value to the Woman's Movement:

> She did not begin the Woman's Movement; nor did she end it. But it was she who gave it passionate, vehement expression, and who poured something of the courage of her own great heart into those of her more timid fellows and induced them, indirectly, to struggle for the extirpation of age-old

conventions that had . . . made the lot of woman painful and frustrated. (p. 218)

Chapter II ('I read and I epitomised what I read'), which deals with the influence of various books on Olive Schreiner's work and the direction of her thinking, is valuable and sound.

She makes a deliberate (sometimes too vigorous) attempt to develop a spiritual interpretation of Olive Schreiner's life and teaching, especially in Chapter VIII, where the main theme is the writer's exploration of truth, and her statements on religion ('There is NOTHING but God', Olive Schreiner once wrote to a clergyman (p. 106)). 'To a strange intensity,' writes Miss Buchanan-Gould,' . . . she added extraordinary spiritual gifts and high moral courage' (p. 54), and this accounts for a great deal in Olive Schreiner.

One striking feature not developed by other biographers is brought out in this book – her overwhelming maternal instinct. 'The nascent maternal instinct of the small girl,' Miss Buchanan-Gould comments, '. . . was to develop into one of the dominant traits of her personality . . .' (p. 30), and it was the 'thwarted maternal instinct which led her, throughout her life, to champion persons or groups who were in any way oppressed' (p. 117). I think this a more defensible interpretation of her desire to champion the underdog than Mrs Friedmann's thesis that Olive Schreiner's was in essence the championship of a child against a sinister mother conception. Another telling judgement is that 'her great need' was 'to give and to receive love unstintingly' (p. 202).

The relationship between Olive Schreiner and Havelock Ellis is more fully dealt with here than ever before – particularly his burning love for her and her curious reluctance to wed him – but the author introduces a very doubtful hypothesis when she asserts that Olive Schreiner rejected Havelock Ellis so that Edith Lees could become his wife. The hypothesis does not tally with the evidence, and Miss Buchanan-Gould ruins an otherwise admirable account of their relationship by so uncritically emphasising this 'secret renunciation'.

OLIVE SCHREINER: A STUDY IN LATENT MEANINGS
by Marion V. Friedmann

This book, although valuable in parts, suffers from a serious defect (like so many theses) – it is an over-simplification. To all, or most of, Olive Schreiner's neuroses, Marion Friedmann ascribes only one cause – her mother. She avers that behind her writing and behind the actions of her life always stood the sinister mother-figure. Statements such as the following seem to me a little high-handed: 'Her revulsion from aggression was partly . . . the feeling-tone of the old struggle, in which the aggressor was always a mother and the victim always a child' (p. 48). There is too much evidence that she is bending the material she uses to support the point she sets out to prove. True, there are those sinister older-women figures in Olive Schreiner's creative writing to be accounted for, but I feel that her by no means consistent attitude to her mother was only a minor contributory factor in their origin. Other women entered her life who wielded as much influence as Rebecca Schreiner; for example the influence of her sister Ettie (at one time a spiritually cramping mentor in Olive's formative years) has hardly any emphasis in Mrs Friedmann's thesis.

Marion Friedmann's approach is neither that of critic nor biographer, but of literary investigator *cum* psychologist. This can be a valid method, but in her treatment of the novels (the only literary work by Olive Schreiner discussed at length by Mrs Friedmann in attempting to prove her thesis) I found it unsatisfactory. This approach does not allow any adequate estimate of Olive Schreiner's work to be made, although it is not Mrs Friedmann's intention to arrive at an estimate ('although I make judgements', p. vii). The contents of the novels are rapidly summarised, the sinister mother-figures introduced, and voice is given to a few sweeping observations. 'If this brief account of its [*From Man to Man's*] 460 pages gives . . . the impression,' she writes, 'that this is a poor novel, that impression is not far off the truth' (p. 14). That her summary does give that impression there is no denying, but it is far from just; it fails to account for the quality of the book's thinking, for its impassioned, but restrained, statements in the cause of feminism, for its quite often vigorous character drawing. Mrs Friedmann was of course interested essentially in tracking down the influence of Olive Schreiner's mother in relation to her life and art, but she should have restricted herself accordingly and not lent herself to dogmatisms about the value of the writer's work.

Her approach is far more successful in the second section, in which she deals with 'The Woman'. This section (in spite of the fact that, like Cronwright-Schreiner, she brings to life the neurotic but hardly the genius) is quite admirable. With beautiful lucidity she accounts for Olive Schreiner's depressions, her asthma, her relationships with women and men, her sexual disposition, and her craving for solitude, love and protection. 'The Woman' is a very valuable addition to the literature on Olive Schreiner, and a guide to future biographers. Interestingly enough, the mother-figure is hardly intruded at all.

The third section, 'Latent Meanings', is a mixture of perceptiveness and unsatisfactory psychological 'elucidation'. Mrs Friedmann's point that 'in Olive's world there was no peace without expiation' (p. 47) has the effect of a shaft of light; it is a penetrating criticism of an aspect of Olive Schreiner's imaginitive writing. But I cannot accept the assertion that 'her reaction to aggression expressed her own aggressive impulses. It seems that we must accept that a process something akin to what the Freudians call "reaction-formation" took place' (p. 50). To use very unscientific terminology, it simply does not take us to the heart of the matter, it does not allow for the emotional ranges of which Olive Schreiner was capable. The following remark also seems to stretch a point:

> Her difficulty in establishing satisfactory relationships with people, her ambivalent attitudes to women, her 'landlady' troubles, all these seem to have resulted from the child's inability to cope with its aggressive impulses towards its

mother. If the psychosomatic investigators are to be believed,
in this same failure lay the origin of Olive's asthma. (p. 51)
Too much in fact has been blamed on the mother, and Marion
Friedmann's thesis tends to totter under its burden.

In the last section, 'The Artist', the psychological references are
occasionally too ambitious for a book of this nature, and they are
not always carried through to their logical conclusions, particularly with regard to Olive Schreiner's own life and writings. However, one point made here, summed up in the following sentence,
provides a clear indication of Olive Schreiner's constitution as a
writer: She was the type of person who '*must* write . . . whether
his basic need is communication or self-expression' (p. 60). Her
basic requirement was neither communication (although writing
was her way of contributing to public issues), nor self-expression
(although this was largely the reason for her creative work) –
apparently she was a born writer (if not always a good one); she
simply *had* to write.

OLIVE SCHREINER: HER FRIENDS AND TIMES
by D. L. Hobman

In writing this biography I think Mrs Hobman should, at least
temporarily, have forgotten she was English: she is so conscious
of this and so ready to defend the English at all times and to discredit the Boers that the balance of her work is seriously disturbed. Instead of attempting to interpret Olive Schreiner's
reasons for the stands she took, and in total disregard of the fact
that she was very honest with herself on public issues, the biographer gives her own opposed views of the rights and wrongs of
various matters with little or no reference to her subject. In the
chapter on the Boer War it is all Mrs Hobman, preparing a careful defence of the English and a denunciation of the Boers, and
very little Olive Schreiner. She was (as her title explains) dealing
not only with Olive Schreiner, but also with her times. But the

account she gives of those times is not objective; indeed, sometimes it is very biased, and for that reason near to valueless. For example, she misses the whole spirit and intention of *Thoughts on South Africa* in her hurry to defend the English people against the writer's strictures. One is justified in taking exception to her inaccurate account of South African conditions, especially those that prevailed at the time of the Anglo-Boer War. For several pages she stoutly attempts to justify the policy of England, and then makes the surprising statement: 'In any case, whether this policy was or was not justifiable . . .' (p. 118) – this makes one suspect that Mrs Hobman had some inkling that she was a vulnerable interpreter of the facts. Several of her remarks strike a discouragingly propagandist note. Her statement that 'the Boers had shattered a very long and very prosperous period of peace, and England was aroused at last' (p. 123), is a grave inaccuracy. Her reference to Afrikaans as 'a shrunken and impoverished Dutch' (p. 116) is a statement made in pure ignorance; but Mrs Hobman makes it with an air of authority. On the other hand, she describes England and the English in honeyed terms; she speaks of their 'heroic splendour' (p. 123) and her (England's) 'beneficent rule' (p. 114). Such terms, deeply felt though they may be, are best confined to the propagandist's handout, and, if used, need very definite critical enlargement. Her description of Rhodes's (possible) boyhood is crudely sentimental ('he had tasted the honey sweetness stored within the enchanted hive of Oxford' (p. 115)).

Because Olive Schreiner, with her courageous idealism and honesty, dared to defend the Boers and to try to explain them, and because she proclaimed what she believed to be true, Mrs Hobman brands her as the enemy and as good as a traitor, and almost attempts to justify the fact that she was pushed from a station platform by a British soldier (p. 123).

I have dwelt at length on this aspect of the biography because I believe it greatly damages a serious attempt at an interpretation of Olive Schreiner's life and work. The biographer may have felt her own patriotism intensely, but Olive Schreiner was her elected subject; her own views on the Boer War and other South African issues should, at least, have taken a distinctly second place. One is even inclined to wonder why she bothered to write the biography, so completely out of sympathy is she at times with her subject.

In her account of Olive Schreiner's friends she tends to dwell on those she made in England, while those in South Africa, with a few notable exceptions, are barely mentioned. Olive Schreiner scarcely features in the chapter on 'Edward Carpenter and his Circle', and from this account one is inclined to wonder in how far she belonged to that circle.

For some unaccountable reason Mrs Hobman is bent on ignoring the existence of Vera Buchanan-Gould's earlier biography. It is not listed in her bibliography, or mentioned by name in her text, although there are several oblique hints that make one feel she could not have been unaware of its existence. Perhaps she rebelled against the uncritical extravagances of that book, but that does not explain her sometimes near farcical attempts to ignore it. 'A suggestion,' she writes, 'that Olive might have sacrificed herself in order that another woman, Edith Lees, could become Havelock Ellis' wife, is improbable' (p. 72). It is hardly likely that she was unaware that this suggestion was made and developed in Vera Buchanan-Gould's biography – but that is the closest reference we have to the previous work. Nor is it likely that she was unaware that Vera Buchanan-Gould had almost certainly established that Olive Schreiner had an early love affair, with a man she wrongly called 'Julius Zaar' (he was in fact Julius Gau, the member of a family well-known to Olive Schreiner in Dordrecht). In describing Olive's early life why does Mrs Hobman write: 'Her unhappiness . . . may well have been due to a passionate love affair with a tragic and humiliating end . . .' (p. 36)? Is she intimating that she is aware of an early love affair, or unaware of it and merely attempting an interpretation of what is unknown? The context of the quotation is unhelpful.

It is a pity that Mrs Hobman's own views on certain issues cripple her work because her attempt in the Introduction at arriving at a just estimate of the woman and the writer has undoubted force. It does not completely succeed, but I think it has taken us nearer than any other piece of writing to the essential Olive Schreiner. 'Her tastes were intellectual rather than aesthetic' (p. 5) is succinctly put, and equally clear-sighted is the statement that in Olive Schreiner we find 'the unending struggle between a rationalist mind and a mystical temperament' (p. 11). Her examination of Olive's difficulty in breathing is the best we have:

> Asthma was . . . to . . . torture her wherever she went. A person of her intense sensibility, full of inner conflict and anxiety, could not but be disturbed in the even rhythm of her breathing; her overstrung nerves were undoubtedly connected with the disease, although whether as cause or as effect can now no longer be ascertained. (p. 7)

The reason for her restless wanderings is also brilliantly pinpointed:

> Like other writers after her – D. H. Lawrence, for instance, or Katherine Mansfield – she was driven from place to place by a sick body and an unquiet mind, always tormented by nostalgia for the undefined. It is no solace to the sufferer that there is no real need for this misery – reason is defeated by a queer compulsion from within. During all her wanderings she must have been searching at least as much for happiness as for health, both seeming to beckon her forever from any spot except the one where at any moment she happened to be. (p. 8)

OLIVE SCHREINER: PORTRAIT OF A SOUTH AFRICAN WOMAN
by Johannes Meintjes

This, the latest, is in many ways the best of the biographies, though in the over-confidence of its assertions and the paucity of its documentation it cannot finally be regarded as satisfactory. A critical, properly documented biography of Olive Schreiner still remains to be written.

In the following passage Meintjes describes the child in front of the mirror in her bedroom:

> A wicked, keen, bright little face would look back at her, as though it belonged to somebody else. (p. 11)

What precisely does this passage represent? Is it an imaginative reconstruction, or is it based on one of Olive Schreiner's own statements about her childhood behaviour? The total exclusion of references leaves us in doubt, and, sadly enough, encourages us to be on our guard against many of the biographer's assertions.

In the same chapter there are some fascinating glimpses of the Rev. Zadock Robinson, but again the descriptions are inadequately documented, and therefore unhelpful to anyone with a serious interest in the subject. Where are the manuscripts? Which of them have already appeared in print? It is quite clear, I think, that Meintjes had access to a wonderful collection of material, much of it unpublished, much of it not accessible even to Cronwright. Why – apart from a few insubstantial references – has he been so reluctant to cite his authorities? Why are we constantly left to surmise what they are? For example, he clearly draws on a valuable document in describing the period in which Olive Schreiner wrote both *Undine* and *The Story of An African Farm*, but only those who know something of the material will recognise the Ratel Hoek Journal, now at the University of Texas, as one of his sources of information. The following:

> I am so weary of this battle; labour on for nothing. In all this great world, there is not one, not one, who is near to me. (p. 37)

is an unacknowledged quotation from the Ratel Hoek Journal. These origins are interesting and would have given far more substance to a work that produces the effect of a patchwork of documentary evidence and semi-inspired guessing.

On what does he base so grave an allegation as the following about the young Olive Schreiner?

> She allowed him [Julius Gau] to seduce her. She missed a period, and she became terrified that she was pregnant. (p. 21)

There may well be a source for this, and one owes it to the world of biographical accuracy to say what it was.

What was his authority for the following equally serious statement about Havelock Ellis and his relationship with Olive Schreiner?

> This then was Ellis's problem: he was impotent. (p. 72)

> They shared a room in Derbyshire . . . They made love, Olive trying to teach him the physical art of love, but with no success. She became more and more frustrated, while Ellis was quite happy to fondle and caress her in 'the glory of nakedness'. He had never known such intimacy with a woman before, and was overcome by the beauty of what he called love play or sex play. He wanted to go on and on, only to be grieved to find that Olive had had enough and that she was not particularly interested in his form of sex play. (p. 73)

Has his record of the secrets of the bedroom been based purely on fact (as his confident tone would seem to imply), or is there in his account a strong element of supposition? The need continually to ask these questions all but destroys the trust he has so persistently been demanding in his reader.

His statements are, almost throughout, this curious mixture of perceptivity and unpersuasive demands on our credulity. Within a single paragraph one finds the following:

> She had dark, very large brown eyes and almost black hair, a height of just over five feet and the Jewish cast of countenance seen in so many of the Schreiner children. Actually no Jewish blood in the family has been traced (Olive would have liked it proved), and a strain of it remains a mere tradition. (p. 12)

> One doubts, however, whether she had the keen assessment of character which some people ascribe to her. (p. 12)

The first statement is concise (despite once again lacking an authority), and the statement about Jewish forbears, including the smile about Olive's wish for them, is very pithy (it owes something to Cronwright's description on page 6 of his biography).

But on what does he base the sweeping assertion of the second statement? The matter is not argued further; rather arrogantly, on his part, it is simply left there. As it is, it remains a grossly inadequate rebuttal of the contention that she *did* have insight into character.

The biographer's assertions seem to become increasingly shrill, and documentary, reasoned support more and more lacking, as he continues. This is evident, for example, when he comes to deal with

> Waldo's description (in his letter to Lyndall) of a man torturing an ox. The brutality of the latter description makes agonising reading, and for Olive, with her passionate feeling for the weak and subordinate, it must have been a purely masochistic indulgence. (p. 57)

The matter again is left there, and must be regarded as inconclusive, even as unfair. There is a more blatant example of this type of thing lower down on the same page:

> That she had bisexual tendencies [rather than 'inverted tendencies'] can be more readily assumed – more or less as the case was with Shelley. (p. 57)

Apart from the fact that they both rebelled against injustice, tyranny and 'general religious concepts', again the matter is left there.

A few pages later one could bring a charge of gross biographical manipulation:

> Before we examine Olive's relationship with Havelock Ellis, it must be stated emphatically that he was not the most important man in her life. Nor was Cronwright. All Olive Schreiner's biographers give this erroneous impression that the two men who meant most to her were Ellis and Cronwright, and this may be because they both wished it to appear so. (p. 60)

This quotation shows the type of assertion that is characteristic of Meintjes. He has his own particular rabbit in the hat, and proceeds to produce it with a flourish. The most important man in Olive's life remains unnamed, and occupies no more than part of the paragraph that follows. Surely this is extravagant, to say the least? What evidence is there, what *documentary* substantiation, for this claim? Let me say straight away that the documents available *do* reveal the presence of such a person, and the masochistic fascination that he aroused in her, but is the price of such a presence the demotion of Ellis, who played a prominent role in her life for nearly forty years, or Cronwright, whom she married? In presenting such an argument, 'importance' would certainly require definition.

The Karl Pearson episode again is made much of by assertion, but insufficiently delineated. When he is not making a bewildering variety of claims, the biographer is much given to woolly thinking. Consider the following description of Ellis:

> As Olive, one can assume without any doubt [?], was the only woman in his life until his marriage at the age of thirty-two, he was certainly not involved with any other woman, although there might have been somebody who wanted him to be. On the other hand this situation might not involve Ellis at all, and it is for this reason that the matter is broached here, and not while describing the problematic stage of their early relationship. (p. 95)

What is all this about? The context does not assist us. One can only guess that he is referring to the 'secret renunciation' made so much of by Vera Buchanan-Gould in her biography, so circuitously avoided by D. L. Hobman, and so emphatically denied by Françoise Lafitte-Cyon in a letter to *The Times Literary Supplement*.[2]

The critical part of this book is undistinguished. The following luke-warm tribute to *Thoughts on South Africa* is characteristic of an attitude that is not reluctant to be patronising, but draws back from any searching analysis:

> For its vivid descriptive matter, its enthusiasm, its powerful style and colourful sweep, *Stray Thoughts* is a book of more than passing interest. (p. 172)

2. Friday, 10th April, 1953.

But I have described this biography as in many ways the best of the five. Where is this quality to be found?

To begin with, the Karoo setting is sparely, beautifully evoked in the opening chapter by someone who clearly knows it well, and someone who has sympathetic insight into its effect on his subject. There is a growing sense of consequence as he describes the impact of *An African Farm* on Havelock Ellis, who had lived for a time in similar surroundings in Australia: Ellis was moved by 'the freshness of its outlook, the firm splendour of its style' (p. 62), and wrote to the young authoress to tell her so. Her reply was charmingly unaffected, yet without a touch of crafty demureness. Indeed, the following shows considerable self-criticism for one so young, and already a successful writer to boot:

> There is too much moralising in the story, but when one is leading an absolutely solitary life one is apt to use one's work as Gregory used his letters, as an outlet for all one's superfluous feelings, without asking too closely whether they can or cannot be artistically expressed there. (p. 63)

(How this tallies with a later assertion is never made clear in the biographer's organisation of his judgements: '. . . he [Ellis] had already realised that she resented criticism of any kind'. (p. 82))

The biographer recalls us to the deep streak of nostalgia in Olive Schreiner for the country she loved:

> The book was written on an up-country farm in the Karoo, and it gives me much pleasure to think that other hearts find it real. I have been now almost three years in England but I long always for that old life. (p. 63)

We know that Olive Schreiner was temperamentally inconsistent, but surely this passage poses a rather effective answer to those fashionable critics[3] who point to the manner in which both South Africa and its 'philistines' appalled her. *Thoughts on South Africa* is, of course, the ultimate answer.

Her contretemps, difficulties, quarrels, clashes, alienation from

3. For example, Dan Jacobson in his Introduction to the 1971 Penguin edition of *The Story of an African Farm.*

117

Ellis, and disenchantment with her husband, point to the over-
bearing tragedy of her life; it was specifically the tragedy of someone who held the belief that

> The older I grow . . . the more intensely it seems to me that
> there's nothing worth living for but love and tenderness
> between human beings. (p. 163)

Johannes Meintjes brings to life the strong spirit that nurtured
itself on the Karoo, and indicates its colossal failure to attain the
high ideals that its loneliness inspired.